SOFT TO

DEDICATED TO THE MEMORY OF

KALAN KAWA KARIM
ALIAS "HOSHYAR" – "AWAKE"

Karim came from Dohuq in Kurdish Iraq. A brave fighter for Kurdish rights, he was shot and wounded by Iraqi troops, and tortured and disabled in Saddam Hussein's jails.

He was granted asylum in the UK and came to live in Swansea with his brother.

He was 29 years old and married.

He was killed by a blow to the back of the neck in a cowardly, unprovoked, racially motivated attack, in the early hours of 6 September 2004 in the centre of Swansea.

His killer, unemployed Lee Mordecai, 27, from Bonymaen, pleaded guilty to manslaughter and was sentenced to five years in prison.

Hafan Books

Hafan: Welsh for sanctuary, refuge, haven

Refugees Writing in Wales Series

Between a Mountain and a Sea (2003) Out of print; texts are online

Nobody's Perfect (2004) ISBN 09545147-18

Soft Touch (2005) ISBN 09545147-34

Each includes poems, fiction, testimony and opinion by 20–30 refugees or asylum seekers and 5–10 other Wales-based writers.

Also forthcoming in 2005, a first collection by a local poet:

My Heart Blown Open Wide by Martin J. White ISBN 09545147-26

All titles £7.50 – or £5 each for two or more – when ordered direct from us (post & packing free). There's an order form at our website: www.hafan.org. Or write to us c/o The Retreat, 2 Humphrey Street, Swansea, SA1 6BG. Cheques payable to "Swansea Bay A.S.S.G." (Don't forget your name and address.)

All proceeds go to Swansea Bay Asylum Seekers Support Group and other refugee charities working with SBASSG.

Swansea Bay Asylum Seekers Support Group

is a constituted voluntary community group, founded in 2001 by local citizens, managed by a committee of seven refugees or asylum seekers and seven others. We provide *drop-ins* every Friday and Saturday: safe spaces; fun for children with professional play workers (funded by Swansea City Council, Interplay Service); free legal advice; informal English classes; tea, coffee, fresh fruit and friendship. We also run *Swansea World Stars* football team (funded by Communities First Trust Fund), who play in Swansea Senior League on Saturdays.

New volunteers and *donations* always needed.

Secretary: Marilyn Thomas – marilyn-thomas@lineone.net

Treasurer: Tom Cheesman – t.cheesman@swan.ac.uk

Co-operative Bank, sort code 08-92-99, *a/c no.* 65063888

Visit **www.hafan.org** for more details

SOFT TOUCH

REFUGEES WRITING IN WALES

3

edited by

Eric Ngalle Charles

Tom Cheesman

and

Sylvie Hoffmann

Swansea
Hafan Books
2005

ISBN 0–9545147–3–4

Cover design by the SBASSG design collective, with special thanks to Tim at the KopyShop, University of Wales Swansea.

Published by Hafan Books   First impression 2005

Hafan Books is a non-profit publisher associated with Swansea Bay Asylum Seekers Support Group (SBASSG) – a community group run by asylum seekers, refugees and other local people.

Hafan Books and **SBASSG** c/o
The Retreat
2 Humphrey Street
Swansea
SA1 6BG

Website: **www.hafan.org**   E-mail: **hafanbooks@yahoo.co.uk**

All proceeds from sales of this book are used to support asylum seekers and refugees through SBASSG, the Welsh Refugee Council, and associated Welsh and UK charities.

The editors thank the contributors, the translators and the unnamed encouragers. All gave their work free of charge.

Printing costs were offset by paid advertisements on the back pages.

This publication was sponsored by Refugee Week Wales 2005.

Designed by Tom Cheesman.   Printed in Wales by Gwasg Gomer.

Contents

Introduction: Persecution?

Tom Cheesman

Afghanistan, Algeria, Bangladesh, Cameroon, Congo-Brazzaville, Congo-Kinshasa, Chile, Croatia, Iraq, Iran, Liberia, Morocco, Pakistan, Rwanda, Sudan, Zimbabwe – people from these and other countries write in *Soft Touch*. What they have in common is that they all came to the UK for the sake of survival. They spoke out against dictatorship, or they worked for human rights groups, or they belong to ethnic or religious minorities regarded as subversive or rebellious, or they refused to fight for a corrupt and oppressive regime – for these and similar reasons they were targeted for persecution. Lucky to be alive, they typically sacrificed everything they owned in order to fund their escape and reach safety here.

To prove that one has been personally persecuted is seldom easy. The Home Office applies strict criteria. For instance, 'persecution' refers only to actions of the state and its forces. It is no good if you have been targeted by a rebel militia (even if it controls a large territory in a civil war). People seldom arrive with a video showing what happened to them. They are assumed to be trying to deceive: aren't they really all 'economic migrants'?

In the effort to keep down the headline figures on asylum applications, and keep up the numbers of refusals and 'returns', the UK government has repeatedly tightened the rules governing asylum applications. Now people can't be accompanied by a solicitor at the all-important first Home Office interview; only five hours of legal aid-funded time are available to solicitors at each stage of application; and no new evidence can be presented at an appeal. There are plans to limit applicants to just one appeal. Given the complexity of many cases and the severe shortage of qualified solicitors, this is a sure recipe for many more miscarriages of justice. And there are also proposals to grant nobody at all permanent residence rights, thus leaving all refugees in a limbo without end.

Applicants who do not submit their application quickly enough after arriving – which means filling out a very long form in English – are considered to have 'failed', without even having a hearing. Many others pass through the system and 'fail' for lack of good legal advice. Most 'failed' asylum seekers cannot be deported, because their countries are far too dangerous for them: the UK would be in breach of international law if we tried to send them back. However, having 'failed', they are entitled to receive no state support whatever – no housing, no benefits – and of course they have no permit to work. They are abandoned to destitution.

Scores of 'failed' asylum seekers in Wales – a constantly growing number – depend on charity for the basic necessities of life. For a place to sleep, they rely on friends, members of faith groups or other sympathetic citizens. Asylum seekers who let them stay on their sofas risk losing their own entitlement to accommodation. Many 'failed' asylum seekers 'disappear' into the illegal job market, where they are vulnerable to exploitation by criminals.

It would be an exaggeration to say that asylum seekers are 'persecuted' in the UK. A constant stream of hostile press reports which encourage the worst popular attitudes and misconceptions – a grotesquely inefficient, under-resourced and prejudicial legal system – detention (with gross mistreatment, as documented in a recent BBC investigation) or accommodation in some of the most deprived housing estates in the country, on a pitiful allowance – laughably inadequate measures to facilitate integration (virtual absence of opportunities to learn English) – and abandonment to destitution – these of course do not constitute 'persecution'.

Despite everything, asylum seekers and refugees are one hell of a lot better off here than in the places they fled from, where they had no life at all to look forward to. And many who have come to Wales have nothing but good things to say about the welcome they have received: they have made friends amongst strangers. On balance, people in Wales can be proud of the way we have helped refugees make new homes and lives here.

So here they are, writing, side by side with their friends and supporters among local poets: writing to express their memories, thoughts and feelings, hoping to be heard as individuals rather than members of a fantasy scary mob, and hoping to help develop a more welcoming and better informed culture in Wales and the UK.

Croeso i bawb! – Welcome, world!

Notes on the Contributors

Eric Ngalle Charles grew up in the small village of Buyea, in Cameroon's South West Province. He left Cameroon in 1997, aiming to join relatives in Belgium, but found himself stranded in Russia. After three years he succeeded in obtaining papers to travel to the UK, claimed asylum, and was granted leave to remain. In Wales he has edited a newsletter for DPIA, given workshops on poetry and displacement in many schools, been profiled in HTV's series 'Melting Pot', and had some poems translated into Welsh for the St David's Eisteddfod, 2002. He is studying for a BSc in Business Information Systems at UWIC and has an Academi grant to complete an autobiographical novel. He has a daughter and a stepdaughter, plays football for Avenue Hotspurs, Ely, and co-founded Les Artistes sans Frontières, a group of refugee poets based in Cardiff and Wrexham.

Tom Cheesman grew up in County Durham. He lived in Germany and France before settling in Swansea in 1990. A lecturer in German at Swansea University, he volunteers with the Swansea Bay Asylum Seekers Support Group. He is married with two daughters.

Sylvie Hoffmann is a freelance artist, storyteller and teacher, and also volunteers with SBASSG. Born in Thionville, France, in 1947, she emigrated to Britain in 1973. In 1978 she was granted indefinite leave to remain. She studied French and English at Birkbeck College, London, and took a PGCE in Swansea. Here she has taught in schools and colleges and worked in cultural projects, such as with Travellers. She has recently worked on radio features about and with destitute asylum seekers, for 'Good Morning Wales'. Sylvie has two daughters, a BA in Architectural Stained Glass from Swansea Institute, a licence to fly, and a GCSE in Welsh.

Mahmood Ahmadifard has a Masters degree in Business and Accountancy from the University of Tehran. Together with his wife and two young children, he was 'dispersed' to Wales in 2003. After more than two years they are still awaiting a Home Office decision on their asylum claim. His poem "Bite the Dust" was written in Farsi; the translation is by the author with Tom Cheesman.

Anahita Alikhani studied Art at the University of Tehran, and worked as a tutor there. In 1998 she began working as a journalist with German, Austrian and Turkish television teams. Detained and tortured after reporting on student protest demonstrations, in 2001 she fled the country and was eventually granted leave to remain in the UK. She has made a film about asylum seekers – *"Anonymous"* – for Valley and Vale Community Arts and for the British Council's A Sense of Place project. She writes and paints while looking for a job.

Abdallah Bashir-Khairi, born on Dagarty Island in the Nile, near Karma, Sudan, studied medicine at Juba University and practised psychiatry in the Sudan and Qatar before coming to the UK as an asylum seeker in 1998. He took an MSc at Cardiff and worked in DPIA's Refugee Doctors Programme and the BE4 project on mental health and social needs among ethnic minorities in Cardiff. His stories have been published in magazines in London and Qatar, where his first collection – *Al-Ruyia* (The Vision) – appeared in 2004. The story published here was translated from the Arabic by Ibrahim Gafar, a philosopher and writer living in London, and edited by Tom Cheesman. Dr Bashir-Khairi left the UK in summer 2004.

Juliet Betts was born in Oxford and studied at the London School of Economics in the 1960s. While bringing up her two daughters, she taught sociology and social policy at a number of British universities and, at one point, in the Caribbean. She moved to Swansea in 2002 and is enjoying exploring pastures new during her retirement.

Byron Beynon's poems have appeared in publications ranging from *The Independent* to *Stand* magazine, *Quadrant* (Australia) to *Planet* (Wales). He co-edits *Roundyhouse* magazine, based in Port Talbot, and is a member of Welsh Poets Against War.

Ian Brown is a writer, creative writing teacher, political activist and recent recruit to fatherhood. He was an aid worker in Africa, the Middle East and South East Asia for twelve years until 1998. He has published books and articles on subjects ranging from the Iran-Iraq war and poverty in Cambodia to corruption in Oxfam, as well as several short stories and a novel. He is now working on his third play dealing with women asylum seekers. "Paying the Price" is a stand-alone piece, written specially for this book.

Humberto Gatica is from Chile. Until his detention in October 1973 under the Pinochet dictatorship, he worked in community arts and cultural projects with shantytown dwellers, peasants and forestry workers. Released from prison in August 1974, with his wife Gabriela he left Chile for Argentina. They came to Swansea as refugees in October 1975. In 1981–84 Humberto worked in a community arts project in a coal mine in Mozambique, returning to Swansea because of the civil war. Since 1987 he has worked as a technician on the Photographic Art BA at Swansea Institute of Higher Education. Occasionally he publishes poetry in magazines, usually Spanish-language publications, and participates in photography exhibitions. The poem "Operating Theatre" describes the time when their baby daughter Andromeda was being treated for cancer at Great Ormond Street Hospital, London.

Hamira A. Geedy is from Mahabad in Iranian Kurdistan. She is a qualified GP: she trained in Shiraz and Tehran and practised for 17 years in Tehran and Mahabad. She is now living in Swansea with her two children and husband, having successfully claimed asylum, but she has not yet been able to pass the language exams which would entitle her to work in the National Health Service. She wrote her story in English.

Soleïman Adel Guémar, born in Algiers in 1963, worked in Algeria as a journalist from 1991. As well as reports and opinion pieces, he also published stories and poems; some poems won national prizes. In 1999 he set up a publishing company and applied for a licence to produce a magazine of investigative journalism. Ensuing threats to his safety persuaded him to leave the country. He suggests his attackers worked for the "military-financial mafia" which runs Algeria, using Islamist extremists as its puppets. Scores of journalists have been killed in Algeria in recent years. Adel applied for asylum at Heathrow in December 2002, was sent to Wales with his wife and three young children, and was granted refugee status in autumn 2004. Some of his poems appeared in *Modern Poetry in Translation* 3/1 (2005); a bilingual collection, working title *State of Emergency*, is in preparation with Arc Publications (Todmorden). Translations by Tom Cheesman and Swansea poet John Goodby.

Imène Guémar is nearly 10. She arrived in Swansea with her family in September 2003, speaking Arabic and French. After only nine months she was given an Award of Excellence by her school as the child "most determined to succeed." Imène enjoys writing in English and playing with words, as well as playing the piano and on the computer. She would like to become a teacher.

Nadji Guémar is seven. He enjoys writing in English, is mad about computers and fascinated with Egyptian mummies, and he would like to become a vet – a "magic doc for animals."

Narriman Guémar, born in Djidjel in 1964, studied electronics and worked in a centre for scientific research specialising in welding and testing. She was a union activist, focusing on women's issues, from 1997 until 2003, when she left Algeria. Translator: Tom Cheesman.

Emily Hinshelwood worked for 14 years in development overseas and in the UK. Now she writes – mainly poetry and plays. In 2003 she won the John Tripp Award for Spoken Poetry. She co-founded the writers' groups Hooker's Pen and Peacock Vein Scriptshop, and scripted the bilingual productions *Dylan Pwy? Dylan Who?* and *Ugain Mlynedd Ymlaen*. Her book *Sucking at Sticky Fingers* won the DSJT Award for the best self-published poetry collection in 2004.

Zhila Irani (pseudonym) has a Masters degree in Chemistry from Tehran University. She is living in Wales with her husband and two young children, awaiting a Home Office decision. She wrote her contribution in English.

Richard Jones: born Nairobi, Kenya, 1947. Polish refugee mother, Kenyan father. Emigrated to the UK, 1953. Emigrated to Wales from England, 1966. Here to stay.

Jelena Jović is 16 and came to Wales from Croatia in 2002. The family's asylum case is still unresolved.

Alhaji Sheku Kamara = ASK is a refugee from Liberia and plays with Swansea World Stars football team.

Dahlian Kirby is a writer and teacher living in Llantwit Major. She has worked and socialised with asylum seekers and refugees in many different situations and places. She currently works part-time in a primary school in Cardiff and is an associate lecturer in philosophy at Cardiff University.

Aimé Kongolo is from Katanga province in Congo-Kinshasa. He was studying child psychology and pedagogy before he came to the UK in 2002, seeking asylum from civil war and ethnic persecution. His case was rejected by the Home Office in November 2003. Since then he has been homeless and destitute. He would like to be studying medicine. He still writes in French but now also in English.

Maxson Sahr Kpakio is from Liberia, where he worked as a freelance journalist for two years, and for the Red Cross and the Human Rights Group. Having fled civil war, he reached the UK and was dispersed to Swansea, where he now lives, with leave to remain. His short drama "It Could Happen to You Too" was twice performed by members of Swansea Bay Asylum Seekers Support Group. He has worked as a volunteer for BTCV, trained as a community worker with the Swansea Council for Voluntary Service, is a member of the Wales Refugee Media Forum's Refugee Link Group, and co-founded the African Community Centre in Swansea.

Showan Kurshid was born in Kirkuk, Iraqi Kurdistan, but had to leave because of the various wars waged by the former Iraqi regime. After years on the run he found a refuge in Sweden, which gave him its citizenship, for which he is grateful. In 2004 he returned to Iraq but was unable to settle and is now back in Wales with his partner and child. He wrote the story published here in English.

William G. Mbwembwe is an asylum seeker from Zimbabwe. He tells his story in "From the South South to the North West".

Michael Mokako lives in Wales with his mother and sisters. They are seeking asylum from Congo-Kinshasa. He knew no English two years ago and is now a strong writer, as well as a passionate basketball player.

Liz Morrison is studying for an MA in Creative and Media Writing at the University of Wales Swansea. Her poems are based on time spent working in Croatian and Austrian refugee camps, 1993–95.

Kamaran Najmadin is from Kurdish Iraq. He and his wife Fatima sought asylum in the UK in 2002. Their application has been refused but they cannot be deported because their country is still unsafe for them. They are living in Wales with no income but luncheon vouchers. He wrote his contribution in English in order to make sure that everyone understands his message.

Alice Salomon is ten, a pupil at St Joseph's Junior School. She got to know asylum seeker and refugee children through her mother's work at the ARC Centre, Portmead, and spends a few hours playing with the children every Saturday at SBASSG's drop-in at St Phillip's community centre. This has made her more confident in life and aware of other people's lives and struggles.

Martin J. White is a naturalist and poet; English, long resident in Swansea and a regular at SBASSG's Friday drop-in. His collection *My Heart Blown Open Wide* will appear with Hafan Books later this year.

Jeni Williams writes regularly on the arts for *New Welsh Review* and *Planet*. She lives in Swansea and teaches Literature and Art History at Trinity College Carmarthen.

What Wales Means to Me

Jelena Jović

Last time you went on holiday, did anyone ask you: "Where are you from?" Probably they did, and when you said you live in Britain, they probably started talking about England. When you say you are not from England they look at you confused, and say: "But you said you were from Britain."

Do you ever get the feeling that we live in one big shadow, England's shadow?

People that do know where Wales is think of it as a small farming country, with lots of sheep and tractors around. These people know nothing about Wales.

It was three years ago that I heard of Wales for the first time, I mean I had heard of the Wales in Australia, but not the one in Britain. Not the one I live in.

Wales has it all – big cities, small quiet villages, national parks, beautiful beaches, valleys and mountains, and one of the most important things: friendly people all over the country.

Did you know that some of the most beautiful beaches are in Wales? Gower, what can I say, amazing beaches. If you see a picture in a brochure, you look at it and think: "This has got to be somewhere in the Caribbean," but underneath it says Gower.

Not many people know of Wales, but to me Wales is everything. It's a beautiful hidden magical place.

What Is It Like to be Me

Imène and Nadji Guémar

About me

Imène Guémar

What is it like to be me?
I'm allowed to go and play by the sea
Just let me find my way

I can do things on my own
I will keep my throat busy
When I'm chit-chit-chatting on the phone
I always get tired and dizzy

English

Nadji Guémar

Write three sentences using the prefix "dis-"

I *dis*like this boy because he beats me up in the playground

I *dis*agree with wolves

I *dis*obey monsters

Tribute to Two Lovely Friends

Alice Salomon

Last night I couldn't sleep. Thoughts ran through my head, I felt hot and tired but I couldn't close my eyes. It all started yesterday when mum told me she had some important news, and I had to be strong and courageous. She explained that my friends M and J had to leave Swansea to go back to their country, Pakistan. Tears came running down my face. Mum gave me a big cuddle and explained that some people coming to live in Britain have to ask permission from the government, and some are successful and can stay, but others have to return to their countries, and although we feel very sad, we have to accept the decision. Mum said that when they come and live in our neighbourhood, we should try to make them feel welcome and share a little of our lives with them.

The memories kept coming all night long. When I met them for the first time, Mum had been invited for tea and asked me to come too. As we arrived, we were greeted by their dad. Their mum was busy in the kitchen. No signs of the girls. Then suddenly we heard some fast steps on the stairs and M appeared in a whirlwind with the biggest smile. Hello, she said in a strong accent, my name is M and I'm very pleased to meet you. I remember thinking how pretty she was with her big brown eyes, caramel-coloured skin and shiny long hair. She was wearing a traditional costume and looked very elegant. Two minutes later her mum came in and I could see two little hands grasping her leg, then a little head appeared and said hello! M was joyful and loud, but J was quiet and shy, probably because she was the youngest. Within five minutes we were playing happily. We had so much fun, M asked her mum if I could stay over. I was busy the next day, so I couldn't, but we arranged to meet regularly.

After a week or so it was half term. I remember we invited M and J to the paddling pool by the seashore at Blackpill, where we played non-stop all day. They invited me over again quite a few times and every time, we had great fun. I remember going to a Halloween party with them, where we all dressed up as ghouls. That was the last time I saw them. A few weeks later, I heard, they had a knock on the door, they were forced to get their belongings and go just like that without time for goodbye.

I can only imagine how they are feeling. I can only imagine the fear of going back, of the unknown. I hope they are OK and they can sleep peacefully. I miss them terribly and thank them for being my special friends.

Mudera

Dedicated to all refugees and asylum seekers in the UK

Alhaji Sheku Kamara = ASK

Yesterday I was woken from my sleep by bombs and gunfire all over my home town. I saw people running up and down, here and there, left and right, east to west. I saw some killed, some injured, and women and young girls raped.

O! the bitter memory of loved ones we have lost and of forced sex by gunmen who claimed to defend us, but killed their own people and forced them to make love at gunpoint.

Boom! Boom! Po! Po! The bombs and gunfire continued, people ran to save their lives. Some swam like fish from one part of the river that was poisoned to the safe part of the river. But he who forced those fish to go back where they came from is worse than he who poisoned that part of the river.

Red! Red! Red! The whole country is painted red with human blood.

Hot! Hot! Fire burning people's houses and property, very hot fire lit by the hawks, like farmers burning the forest to start farming.

The clouds were covered by smoke, people ran to save their lives. Some flew like birds from a burning tree to a safe one. But he who caught a bird and plucked its wings and sent it back to that burning tree is a murderer. And that big strong eagle who chased that little peaceful bird from its nest and left it homeless is heartless.

O! poor bird flying from east to west searching for a tree to pass the night, don't worry, no matter how long it rains or snows the sun must shine again and dry your wet clothes and keep your cold body warm. Then you will be able to thank almighty God and all the good people who helped you through.

A Silence

Emily Hinshelwood

They took my dress when I came here
the cotton stained with yesterday's tear
and red with the blood of my mother

They took the bandage from my frostbitten feet
the dirty rag
a sheet
that belonged to my brother

And in my head my memories fly
of Lhasa in flames, of dust in the sky
the policeman pulling my mother's hair
her mouth was screaming, her legs were bare

They spoke to me in a foreign tongue
their eyeballs stared, their shouting stung
as they scribbled on their form

Gave me water in a plastic beaker
issued vouchers for an asylum seeker
and stuck me in this children's dorm

And in my mind my memories race
my burning home, my aunt's dead face
the escape I made up the mountainside
the shameful payment I made to the guide

They took away my dignity
my vanity
my sanity

But in my head my mind recalls
the wheels of prayer, the coloured shawls
my baby sister's laughing face
my mother's strength, my father's grace

And though they say it'll damage my health
I'll keep my memories to myself
because they are
as I can see
the one thing they can't take from me

From the South South to the North West

William G. Mbwembwe

I come from a land way down in the south – though it's a small country, it's bigger than the islands of Great Britain. This is where the winters are not as cold and the summer is just too hot. I mean damn, that place is hot. Sometimes the cold is good coz it keeps you moving, but when it's seething hot, all you wanna do is get some shade and snooze off.

I was born privileged but not very. We lived in a low density suburb for the upper middle class. I was a manager in a small company that made tons of cash money, I had my own house, my own car plus company car. So what the hell am I doing in this place living on NASS handouts?

Well ...

It was a sunny Saturday afternoon and here we were. Anybody who was somebody met here on the weekend, some to show off their latest acquisitions, be it a new car or a new girl. This is kwaMereki in downtown Harare. We met here for a braai (bar-b-q), and Amai Gringo or any one of the ladies would make sadza (that's maize-corn mash, Shona-style). Even though the sadza looked suspect healthwise, it sure did taste better than the one the missus made at home. Some brought their families, which I felt was out of place, this was the big boys' play area. Even though beer was drunk outside, the police didn't bother anybody. As for plumbing – behind your car would be good enough, but of course for the serious stuff you'd have to go home.

Anyway, on this particular afternoon we were there as usual and music was blaring from the speaker on the door of one of the bottle stores and I still remember Eddy Grant's "Gimme Hope Jo'Anna" being played more than once. What irony coz on this day we were talking politics. This was April

2000 and the last six months had brought too many changes. The government felt threatened. A new political party had everybody singing its name, the government's draft constitution had been rejected by the people, and elections were just around the nearest corner. The government decided to go on the African type of offensive, beat everybody into submission. The main spy agency, the CIO, was working overtime. I didn't see the unmarked police car, I had gone to do the plumbing thing a few cars away, but I finished in time to see my "political analysis and debate team" being bundled into the car and I knew it would be wiser to head home.

Reports of people being tortured or killed were in the papers daily, man it was ugly, this was no scary movie this was for real, but of course it was happening elsewhere so I did not panic. But when the invaders invaded the farm across the road and started demanding food and water, I knew vamoosing was the best advice. We packed up all our stuff including the roaches (you don't leave those behind – they are family), and we headed off to live somewhere else (which I won't say coz I don't trust you).

The house I had left behind, in the months before and after the elections it was ransacked. Neighbours told me that the 'visitors' came two or three times a week in the dead of night, maybe so they can find me home – but why me? I ain't done nobody no harm, I'm just an honest citizen with an honest job trying to make an honest living. Yes I do have opinions, but so does everybody else and lemme tell you something, my opinion is like a drop in the ocean, it don't require late-night visitations for clarification and besides, I only air my views to friends and family and I don't even think anybody cares what I say. You see, where I come from in the southern part of Africa, late-night 'visitors' cannot be reasoned with nor can one negotiate with them, when you see them do the va-va-voom and don't look back ...

I took a late lunch break one day and as I was enjoying my lemon'n'herb quarter chicken from Nando's and a milkshake from Creamy Inn, my phone rang and it was the boss himself. He told me not to come back to work that day and not even in the near future, he was going to send someone with my stuff to where I was right away. The anger that consumed me was unmentionable – after all I was the most hard-working and my department was flourishing, in fact a few weeks earlier I had gotten a raise. I couldn't finish my food. However when the messenger arrived and told me the full version, anger turned to fear. I was literally shaking – the 'visitors' had come to my workplace.

What? How? When? You know the one-word questions you ask in such situations. I knew I had to get outta there and fast so we withdrew all our savings and without telling a soul, not even mom and dad, we landed at Gatwick Airport.

Asylum Seekers: Prisoners

Zhila Irani

Words have different meanings in different situations. Take the word 'home', for example. In your own country, 'home' means the place you live, but when you're a refugee, 'home' means motherland, freedom, family, language, respect, safety, neighbours, life .... If you lose such an important thing, no benefits can ever make up for it.

That's why an asylum seeker is a prisoner: a prisoner has no home, no refuge. Life is like a prison when you cannot be happy, when you have to start from zero, when all your experience, your education, even your language is worthless. Asylum seekers are prisoners, alone and with no one to understand them.

In Iran, we had no idea what an asylum seeker is, or what they go through. We had well over a million refugees from Afghanistan. They first came more than thirty years ago, when the Russians invaded their country. Generally, they had few problems, having almost the same language, culture, religion, customs and physical features as Iranian people. They were able to live and work – in fact they had almost everything except Iranian nationality.

Then, after many years, the Russians left Afghanistan. Most of the refugees went back. We were surprised, since it was far from safe. But they said: "This is not our country; Afghanistan is where we belong." So they took all their belongings and went back.

The Taliban were in control, and when these people came, they took all their possessions off them, even took the wives and daughters, and forced the men to enlist in the army, saying: "We had to fight for years, now it's your turn!" So those who were able to flee, fled once again, back to Iran.

Now, when we came to this country, we realised that when you are a refugee, or an asylum seeker, people do not recognise you, or understand you, or believe you, or respect you. If you have had to flee because you have been protesting against the regime, in the name of human rights, nobody believes you. You have to prove everything, and it's not easy. And nobody realises what it's like to be housed in the worst part of the city, with no choice about where you live, no choice about where your children go to school, and forbidden to work, waiting years for a decision on your claim for asylum.

When you flee your country, you lose your past, and you lose your future too.

A Home for the Lost (Two Poems)

Liz Morrison

A live grenade

A live grenade lies
a stone's throw away.
From my friends Adele and Samira.

A home for the lost

A brother slaps another brother
looking out for one another.

Bombs drop as soldiers attack.
Fathers lost, buried en masse.

Widowed mothers standing hopeless,
hot, cross tears blurring their focus,

packing toys, pants and socks
finding a home for what's not lost.

The mother's son hits another's son,
one war is over, another begun.

The Angelic Faces (Two Poems)

William G. Mbwembwe

I guarantee

I guarantee that you will be safe going to Zimbabwe
But I cannot guarantee your safety when you get there
I can guarantee that there is freedom of speech in Zimbabwe
But I cannot guarantee freedom after your speech
I can guarantee, all basic commodities are in plenty supply
You only have to read the paper and listen to the news
I can guarantee, the rate of crime is very low in Zimbabwe
Everybody is into it, it's the norm
I can guarantee, fuel is plenty-plus in Zimbabwe
Always at a filling station at the other side of town
I can guarantee free and fair elections in Zimbabwe
You are free and have a very fair chance
To vote for the ruling party
I can guarantee you a long life in Zimbabwe
Just don't carry this poem around with you.

(March 2005)

The angelic faces

Melancholy, that's the word
There ain't no joy coz it's all so sad
The evil, the ugly and the very bad
So don't start with me coz this makes me mad

But if it is love, then why do we run away
And why would I be here today?
It is purely evil when you smile
When the children go hungry, and when they cry

"They colonised us ..." is an old Chimurenga song
Coz this is wrong, this is so wrong
Even being forced to sing "Pamberi ne" just to get the daily feed
You're like a goodly apple with a rotten inside

When there ain't no cash you say let's talk
Let there be a bumper harvest – you tell me to walk

I wanna know, so tell me pliz
How do you feel when you see all this?
And after you're through with all your analysis ...
How 'bout the children ... the angelic faces?

Chimurenga (a Shona word) refers to the struggle against colonisation.
"Pamberi ne ..." ("Forward ...") is a Zanu PF propaganda song.

State of Emergency (Six Poems)

Soleïman Adel Guémar

State of emergency

1

army boots kicking my face in
fingernails torn out one by one
skull savaged by a drill
militia-men at my bed
in shifts until morning
awaiting the order to slit my throat
avidly

2

guilty of having puked
out the window of a packed bus
over the limo of a general
of the Popular Democratic
Republic of Algeria
guilty of being hollow-eyed
of being grief-stricken
my heart in flames
I am guilty of being horrified
by all the massacres crimes
against humanity committed
unpunished at my door

3

Tizi mourns its citizens shot
mown down daily
countless uncounted

I am still colonised
filed in triplicate
humiliated and tortured
flung in jail for having ideas
executed point-blank
massacred under floodlights
behind closed doors all night long
a few steps from a barracks
under the blank gaze of generals
I return to the elements
at the bottom of an old well

– the artificially incubated
fundamentalist ogre
makes a show
of his bloodsoaked fangs –

4

Algiers betrayed
ordered to the electrodes
adopts a posture
which is foetal

The festival of the wolf

hands in my pockets
I was walking along the rue Ben M'hidi
it was a day of mizzle and the sunlight
was spurting out between the clouds
I had no need
of umbrella
of car
of lovers' tryst
to be happy
I simply wanted to drink
a cup of black coffee near the port
and gaze out facing the sea
but that day
ships in the harbour hid the horizon
crows were cawing on the rooves
a vague hubbub was rising from the town

they hadn't yet fired on the crowd

Gégène

these lost eyes
this shaven skull
these broken teeth
this nose which bleeds

this naked body
is sat
on the neck of a bottle

Riffraff

far from the bunkers where the riffraff
in or out of uniform sprouts
where the hysteria
is only matched by that of bitches
on heat
far from this shit
that kills
children dream of exile
in the slums
and cry vengeance !

do you hear them ?

Evenings

there are evenings when I laugh loudly
when the people opposite are out
and other terribly sad evenings
I drain – dry – rivers in spate
and lob – zoop ! – glasses – crash ! –
through the skylight onto the mad dogs

there are evenings when the dead dogs
scratch at my door seeking vengeance
and other far calmer evenings
I listen to old mosquitoes dancing
around stains of lost blood
on the sofa of my romances

there are evenings when the people opposite
speak about flowers and suns
digging trenches the length of their dreams
as far as the horizon
there are evenings when I feel like
wearing – oof ! – gas masks

Eternal

blindfolded
the beach is dirty
the sea is swollen
the gulls fly low
the wind's not ill
the catches clink dull
I want to go home
I just saw their mugs
– they're so ugly mother ! –
they shaved my skull
– it's to kill the lice –
they've even given me
a smart outfit all in red
so it won't stain
the gulls fly low
the catches clink dull
it might be time now
I'm ashamed I'm so scared
blindfolded

Bite the Dust

Mahmood Ahmadifard

message from cold silent history
along the path of time
from a hard time
like a spaceship
penned in by night
a beam of light
among the stars
make your way
let light be our desire
find a captain
escape the darkness
morning comes
those who choose freedom
over evil
those who choose to bite the dust
over living a lickspittle life
a time machine
among ruins
no bread
pain in
orphan eyes
seekers of utopia
show yourselves
find a leader
gather for strength
clasp hands
wherever whenever tyrants
steal freedom
let them know we are there

The Defeated (Four Poems)

Aimé Kongolo

Sans titre

There is war in my blood
This war
In my blood
War which I was born
With

The lost birds

You lost birds, remember you are on hopeless trees.
All fruits were taken and you know it, but it's shameless.
You live a black life, hopeless.

You lost birds with a black past,
Your present is in darkness
And blackness drapes your souls.

O black birds on black trees,
You have no wings to fly.
Looking out to see where hope will come
Your hope is without dignity.

The Defeated

Walking in fear. Our bones burnt on the ways.
Frightening bombshell on the earth.
Counting hopelessly how many days
The red sea will stop flowing from the north.

Eagles flying over mountains,
Brave men leaping like springbok in the deserts,
Eagles pacing loud along seashores.
We drew back in blindness, we walked in clammy crypts.

Stormy and rebel waves wiggling by,
Heroic eyes dried up between mountains,
Shamed streams carried away by storms,
Bent necks stiffened to turn backs on light.

Brave men's flags frozen in their waving.
Public hands flagged and gummy.
Brave men passed by, soldiers without flags.
And our existence vanished into air.

Amour lointain

It's a wagon of love flowers
Adrift on the happiness ocean of love
The Titanic of all lovers
Pushed by the immense wave of love –
So beautiful! So far –

It implies pain and joy at once –
Open your eyes and look out –
The deep breath and hostility –
The strain of love which asks to be accomplished
And one cannot exist without the other –

So far! Fleeing the suffering –
Suffering is part of love –
There resides the mystery of loving –
I hold you with a heart of love
Like the credo of a sexless monk
But remember the time of loving –

So beautiful! So far – but it's love –
You plant me in an autumn garden
Water me with faraway tenderness wave –
But remember the time on love's lawn
Where all lovers' happiness resides –

The scent of a rose –
The breathing of love's flowers –
A respiration aspiration inspiration –
One breathing with another – forever –

So beautiful! So far, but it's love –
Happiness is only part of love –
But it's a feeling you must learn –
There, they will say I love you!

The First Fear

Aimé Kongolo

Tourra, bereft of the convictions that had accompanied all his past, had abdicated the centre of his life and was the more mortal for it.

The country was entering a period of rest after seven years of civil war. The war-weary population dared to hope that peace had finally come to their land. Seven years before, Tourra had left Kivu in fear of the rebel airforce that took his family to the gardens of death. When the young man returned to Kivu, old Mrs Farabin, his neighbour, reminded him that he did, after all, belong 'somewhere'.

The changes during this time were immense, but as a professor of politics, Tourra could see that the government was not fulfilling its role. The politics he was teaching showed that the government's behaviour had not changed. In fact the situation in his country was deteriorating. People were disillusioned. Corruption and injustice were rife at all levels. The country was fertile ground for rebel troops. Although occasional skirmishes were quashed by government forces, they were gradually intensifying.

It was three o'clock in the morning and it was the coldest night Tourra had ever known. He always awoke at the same time, since first going into exile. The darkness was tomb-like; he could see neither trees nor streets nor was there natural peace; he heard guns banging, banging to the north of the city, and heavy bombing. He did not want to ignore the sound, nor to suffer it, but he knew his country to be a garden of death. He had just enough beats in his heart. "How can my heart have been strong enough to give me new life?" he asked himself.

The government forces had still not yet managed to oust the rebels. They were advancing further up the main road towards Kivu, in the eastern part of the Democratic Republic of Congo.

Tourra heard more gunfire, and then the terrifying booming of an anti-aircraft gun. Suddenly his heart was beating and beating. The beating of his heart was not only in his heart, it went through his head. His blood felt hot, and his breathing was as hot as a volcano blasting water into steam.

And somebody knocked at the door! Knock, knock! For some seconds, Tourra was like an Egyptian mummy. All he could think was, don't open the door, jump through the window! But the room he lived in had no window. Can I hide under the bed? he asked himself. But again, there was no 'under the bed'. High-pressure anxiety ran through his body. He was perspiring as if rain were pouring over him.

After all these years, he said to himself, I haven't taken the time to practice the skills of men. He knew one person in the town who never appeared exhausted or disheartened. That was what gave him strength. Emotions and passions familiar from his first exile aroused Tourra now. It was not faintheartedness nor fear of death, of bombing or heavy guns, which stopped him from opening the door: first and only, it was the fear of being taken away to serve in the army. He could remember what had happened seven years ago, when all the young people were forced to carry arms to defend the government.

Minutes later, old Mrs Farabin came to knock on the door too. He heard her talking to somebody, then she shouted: "Tourra! Tourra! Tourra!"

At the third call, he answered. "Who is it?" he asked with a cold but mild voice.

"It's me! It's me, Mrs Farabin!"

Tourra decided to open the door. He saw Mrs Farabin and his cousin, Neron, who said: "They're coming this way!"

"Who are coming?" he asked.

"The rebels!" answered Neron.

"Since when are you so timid?" asked Mrs Farabin.

"Uh, well, just for this moment, not all my life," Tourra replied.

For a long moment, he kept asking himself a question, over and over again. Finally he asked Mrs Farabin: "So, this is the *somewhere* you said I belong?"

She failed to answer, only crying and crying, on and on, saying: "It's my fault!"

Tourra decided to go away. When there is war in this country, the government takes young people to be soldiers. "To be a soldier is not my destiny, not all my life," he said. To be a soldier, he knew, is all about killing, just as his family had been killed.

He decided to run away from the town into the bush, where he found himself right in the rebels' camp. "Look, a new recruit! Welcome! Well, well! What disgrace! Our enemy is mistaken!" – this was the rebels' greeting to him, for Tourra did not belong.

Tourra could move neither forward nor backward. It all happened in darkness, and in darkness his name was shrouded in sudden mystery. His eyes glazed over. He never saw the sun nor knew anything else from there on. Even if he could have lived a thousand years, twice over, he would fail to be remembered. What is good and what is bad in a man's life? His few and meaningless days, Tourra passed through them like a shadow.

To be free in spirit is the destiny of every human being – the living should take this to heart! Free in soul and free in spirit!

Watching Gavras's *Missing*

Richard Jones

Advice before entering a makeshift mortuary in Santiago.

1. Wear warm clothing
   to prevent excessive shivering.

2. Tread carefully
   whilst negotiating the bodies.

3. There is no need to look down at first
   as all of these have already been identified.

4. Note how efficiently
   bodies have been displayed.

5. Some bodies
   have yet to be determined.

6. When necessary, use the framework of the
                                    iron staircase
   to support yourself whilst searching for your own son.

7. Some corpses have been spread over the skylight
   to block out intrusive light.

8. Leave the cinema during a cloudburst.
   This will help wash away the tears.

9. There is no known remedy
   for this knowledge.

Shadows of a Dream (Three Poems)

Humberto Gatica

The emigrant

neither
shipwrecked
nor a traveller
rather he is
a shattered man
knocking on
illusory doors
expending
his desperate
and obscene
language
secretly
erasing
his nightmares
and waking
every morning
surrounded
by labyrinths
and broken dreams

Shadows of a dream

there is a city
coming again
and again
to my dreams
trapped
under a dark sky
and a grey landscape
this is a city
transforming itself
all the time
where the streets
turn
into rivers of mud
and the hills open
deep precipices
in whose walls
water runs
slowly
like tears
in this city
buildings move around
changing places
in this deserted city
i appear
like a survivor
of a tragedy
i do not remember
looking for something
i have already forgotten

Operating theatre

In memory of Andromeda Eloiza

Downcast I walk along Southampton Row
dreaming that I draw near
to the bright shining density
of the next century
believing that the universe
in spinning round
is wearing thin on its darker side
and that death
is an eye vanishing into the secret sleep of eternity.
Tiny phantoms terrified by paranoia
snort and spring under the falling snow.
Green nightmares billow under the magic
weight of rotating crosses.
Hysterical spotlights
bulging eyes
alcoholic solitude
everything as in a dream.
Walled-in balconies telling us that
the emptiness is an illusion.
Brightly-lit corridors where
golden-haired angels dance demented
with their hypodermics.
Roads that are cold so that
the planet may bleed.
Alone I wander
knowing the simple joy of finding a lavatory
while my child wastes away
in the glacier dream of anaesthesia
my little one
with her wide open eyes

howls into a backyard
of thriving rubbish
and the VINCHRISTIN
is a lost jet thick with terror and vomit
CYCLOPHOSPHOMIDE the same
and ACTRYMYACINE and and and

Heathrow
Heathrow
puritan labyrinth
in a cannibalistic fever
where defenceless hopeful pilgrims
beat themselves against the walls of illusion
while the bright towers of glass boil
under a sky worn away by slogans.

I wander in anguish along Southampton Row.
The evening is crumbling
blackened by strident noises.
In Pullinque
mother
silent
a Fellini-esque half-century
of hypochondria and rheumatism.
The horizon
is a bottle of serum
incessantly beating upon
the rafters of the night.
A nurse smiles
and sings
in front of us
and we still shocked
by that skeleton
too young

who first appears then disappears
begging and terrified
on the dim screen of the closed-circuit tv.

Lighthouses broken in order not to alter
the oceanic dream of the storms.
Old proverbs to confront new life.
Punctual ambulances speeding
straight for nothingness.
Cobalt bombs.
Tyrannical masks.
Cosmic sound.

Perhaps this evening
I will call someone
someone who will answer me
from mental sketches of the future.
There are no birds in Southampton Row
but Southampton Row is full of nostalgia
and arrogance.
And the Doctor
what will the Doctor say tomorrow?
Ah my little girl
tomorrow is like a meteorite
fleeing from your door.
White pieces of evening-time London
disintegrate before your window.
I see you going all alone
into the oxygen tent
embraced only by
your three and a half
years of reality.
The city is an electric limbo
roaring like a sawmill.

The singer's cellophane throat
is bleeding. The civil
servants and machines float
docile and tragic
like a space station
and once again death
becomes our travelling companion
once again the many and the few
gallop away
each to their own infinity.
Every day
I search for you among the sacred trees
of the cosmic forest.
I need your voice
to speak to me of the mystery
the symmetry of infinity.
Till then
I explain to you that the world
goes on turning
further and further from paradise
its half-awake tango.

Local Therapy

Soleïman Adel Guémar

Contrary to the meteorological prognostications, the weather was superb.

Omar stretched feverishly, cracked his ten fingers one by one as if in a spirit of revenge (a habit which had once earned him enraged reproaches and punishments from his schoolmasters), then contemplated the furtive trails of white clouds following one another in single file and disappearing behind the dead angle of his window.

"I'm a bird!" Omar said to himself as he slid out of bed at the same time as his shadow. He went straight to the bathroom and inadvertantly turned on the tap. A flood of creepy-crawlies, the same ones that haunted him by night, filled the basin. He turned the tap off again and one-two-three, on tip-toe, crossed the twenty tiles which separated him from his bed.

Strange whisperings, punctuated by sudden sounds of shouting and breaking glass, emanated from the large lizard on the ceiling. Car-horns had taken over from the morning cooing of the pigeons. The streets had been invaded by a curiously silent crowd, utterly timorous due to the lack of interrogations.

Bodies misshapen by virtue of reason bowed very low to the scarecrows placed here and there on the pavements and actually went down on all fours when dignitaries hidden behind dark glasses and smoked glass windows passed by occasionally.

"Just before the dignitaries belch into the microphones," sighed Omar, "they stuff themselves. Patriotically! To make sure that the rest of humanity never has time to guess the dish of the day." And he watched them as they lied, without batting an eyelid, all down through the generations. "The rest of humanity is a clapometer!" Omar confided to his shadow, who was indifferently munching the piece of nougat which, the night before, had dropped from the pocket of the matron on guard. Omar had had more than one opportunity to kill her. He certainly would have done so, if she had not been so pretty. And it wasn't the daily injection of a concentrated dose of phenobarbital that stopped him. All was still clear in his mind. Despite the lobotomy which he had been made to undergo on the very day he was admitted. The doctor in charge had said: "That's one less quibbler!"

The drill had left practically no scar. It might have been a beauty spot on his forehead. Over the years, three long hairs had sprouted around it. Three years, three hairs. The equation of his internal clock.

He did sometimes bang his head on the walls, on the bars of the window, for the ticking had become unbearable. "Apparently, in cages, wild beasts kill themselves that way," his shadow always pointed out.

Omar had to calm down once and for all. The instructions were clear. "Double the dose of creepy crawlies, triple it! No more kidding around!" the doctor ordered. The matron on guard obeyed. Omar cried: "I'm a bird!"

Two tugs were sticking to the sides of a cargo ship returning to port. In the evening, the television had announced bad weather for the following day.

The Ladders of Ascent and Continuity

Abdallah Bashir-Khairi

The deep furrows which Time had engraved into the old man's forehead were deepening yet. With the tribal tattoos on his cheeks, the old man's face appeared quietly calm, solemn and spiritual. He had long been on his sick-bed, but none of his sons were near him to keep him company. This caused him great sadness. The shadows of their robust bodies stretching away at dusk towards the east, the echoing voices of sheep and cattle across his farmland, were memories. His sons had abandoned the land as its revenues no longer sufficed to abate hunger. Time had ceased to be personified. Everything, from the shimmers of the sea to the sun, was disintegrating.

He kept sorrowful memory at bay. The knotted cords connecting him with these valleys and plains were fraying. He strove to drive the very image of what had been lost from his memory. Not only had his sons crossed the sea, their mother that afternoon had performed her last ablution and chosen to go – with a last, gentle sigh before taking to her death-bed. The old man turned a rosary in his hand, which reminded him of the turning water wheels, once so affluent with water. He saw everything now as if taking final leave, and his eyes told what he glimpsed of the future's stories. *"Oh my sons, he who has missed the goodness of these river-banks has missed plentiful goodness!"*

But sons and fathers have marked out distances between themselves, and even their languages have altered beyond intelligibility.

In the background, the sound of the women wailing for the old man mingled with the voices of the small dams in the night of the island. The youngest son had been travelling to the city on

51

some business of his own. But the news of his old father's death reached him on the way. So he came back at once, bemoaning the hard luck that had made him travel at that very time. Time was now saying its own farewell to the lands of youth. The son sat on a rock at the high end of the *maseed*. It was as if his tears could not express his loss and sadness. On his way to the city he had been apprehensive about his father, and his heart had often told him to return, but the bright dancing phantoms of the city, in his imagination, had distracted him.

From his seat, there on that rock, his back to the sun setting behind the palm trees, he forgot the wailing in the background and submitted himself to the sight of the shadows extending to the east. Was this the life of the old man, at the moment when the Unknown veiled him in its fog: a shadow over the earth?

When he came back to himself, he felt like one who has travelled far into his innermost recesses, while staying immersed in the tranquil climate of that place. He felt as if he had entered into a prayer – he, or the many selves within. The still-expanding shadow was a noble sadness, into which his father had travelled. But he had left behind for the son a cup that overflowed. The stations of death – beware! – are many! But the nearest we do not even perceive, until there comes such a catalyst as this father's death. For the sheikh had died like one who knows when the hand of fate will suddenly fall on him, as if he had chosen an authentic moment of solitude in order to have an intimate encounter with death.

The ancient books transcribed with blue-black ink showed both the calligraphic signs of the father and the legacy of the ancestors. The son loved their ancient fragrance. So, lost in reveries, his soul persuaded him to get up and go to sit beside these manuscripts, which were kept alongside the great box called *assahhara*, with its contents of a sword in its sheath, some copper plates, a pitcher that had been brought from Egypt, and a plate named *silam*.

First the birds, then the young boys announced the beginnings of dawn on the island. They distracted the son's attention from the ink's lines. How he would have liked to remain bent over them by the lantern's faint light! River cranes were flying over the waters between the little islands, followed by their young. There is no better resting-place for the soul. The whole scene is of overlapping images, small dams, water cascading, little and big birds' wings visiting water in light-spirited journeys. Now the son was made aware that his inner being was becoming both a passage-way and a dwelling-place. His father's departure did not demand the usual grief. The sons had wandered into the chasms of lands beyond the sea, and not one of them had come back. But the father who had said, *"Oh my sons, he who has missed the goodness of these river-banks has missed plentiful goodness!"* – the father had departed, yet still dwelled in those who lived in peace.

As the son grew up, the father's features matured in him. He became the image of him – just as he had been created and given form. At first nobody noticed – and anyway, what is surprising about it?

Nevertheless, why should it be that, with every new day, the people sensed the father in the son amongst them? The same calmness, the same solemnity. It was as if he had come back to them, weaving anew the garments of youth. Stranger still, people said that anyone who sat with the son enjoyed seasons of fertility and plenty, just as was said of the father. Those gifted with a lively imagination said that the father's leaving and the son's return had been synchronized 'beat by beat', in a rhythm measuring the pace of Time immemorial.

Some spoke of this with gladness, others with astonishment. One perceptive observer implied that when the son reached the age at which the other sons had left, if those sons then came back, they would be certain to think the passing of the father merely an illusion: he who had died would be the son!

The son has not been created anew. So why would something about him remind everyone not just of the father's features, but of his temperament and soul? It was as if a mystery initiated by the father had transcended life and death so as to remain eternal in the son.

The father's Quranic chanting returned to the drought-plagued land, and in the space of two seasons made it green again. The chanted tune seemed to be flowing not only from the vocal cords through the tongue and lips, but from the whole body. And it was as if many little children, clad in billowing shawls, were dancing in circles around the tune and then each of them carrying it, on their wings, to a different destination. So the tune opened a door into the wall of the children's familiar time, envisioning a green pavillion gently leading to a paradise. "*Oh my sons, he who has missed the goodness of these river-banks has missed plentiful goodness!*"

maseed: traditional Quranic school

My Daughter, Your Mother

Juliet Betts

Just as the kettle boiled, the doorbell rang. That would be her neighbour Betty – no one else much came to her door these days. May opened the door and Betty bustled in. "Can I get you any shopping from the village this afternoon? Mind you, I don't know whether I'll find anything we want down there. It's like somewhere foreign these days, all those Asian shops with funny vegetables and fruit on the pavements. It all looks so scruffy." "Would you like a cup of tea?" May managed to ask between Betty's chatter. "Oh yes please. When you think what it used to be like, you remember, May? Browns the butcher's, and the greengrocer's, and that lovely bakery ..."

May made the tea. Yes, she thought, it really was like a village in those days. Betty followed her into the sitting room. "And have you seen the new people in the Post Office? Another Asian couple have taken over now – the woman wears all that black from head to foot. I bet they don't speak proper English. I don't know what happened to that nice Mr and Mrs McFarlane. Such a shame – they were always so helpful. I wish we had another Post Office to go to." "Well, I've got to go there today whether I like it or not," said May as she offered Betty a biscuit.

The Post Office looked the same from the outside. As May opened the door to step in, her foot caught on the step and she stumbled. She held out a hand to save herself, but the heavy bag in her other hand pulled her down. She felt herself collide with the floor. Then she grew faint. After what seemed like hours, she heard a door open and close, running feet coming near, a voice saying: "Are you all right? Let me help you." Black robes swung past her face and a woman knelt down next to her. "Are you all right?" she repeated. "Can I help you get up?" The woman held out her arms and helped May gently to her feet. "You must come and sit down. I will make you a cup of tea. You have had a terrible shock." May allowed herself to be walked slowly to a room behind the Post Office counter. The woman helped her to a soft chair and put her foot on a stool. Before May closed her eyes, she saw a room that was simply furnished in warm colours: reds, browns and gold. On the wall was wooden plaque with strange writing on it. Soon there was a cup of tea in her hand. Her calf hurt and she knew she would be badly bruised.

She opened her eyes. "Where's my parcel?" she asked anxiously. "Don't worry, it is safe. I will post it for you now, but first, please let me call the doctor for you." "In a minute, maybe. But the parcel's for my daughter in America. For her birthday." "Oh, you have a daughter in America? Does she have a family there?" "Yes, she has a boy and a girl. She's been there a long time." As May spoke, she could feel her tears beginning to flow. How stupid, she said to herself, and in front of a stranger. "Oh, I know how hard that is," said the woman. "I cry often for my mother in Afghanistan. When we left we could not bring her with us. I've not seen her for so many years. I miss her terribly." May felt herself allowing the woman to take her hand. "You must miss your daughter too. How long has she been there?" "Oh, over thirty years. I try not to think about it." "I know my mother misses us too. But we had no choice, we had to leave our home and family."

May was silent. She opened her eyes and looked at the young woman. She was struck by the pale brown of her skin and the kindness of her eyes. Having her hand held was so comforting. Her leg was hurting but her mind was elsewhere. Suddenly she asked, "What do you mean, you had to leave?" "The Russians came and bombed our city," the woman replied. "Our home was destroyed. There were gunmen on the streets.

Everything was in chaos. We tried to live normally and stay together as a family, but it was impossible. My husband was a teacher, but no one was being paid anymore. He was in danger from the regime so our families put all their money together to help us to leave."

"It sounds like the Jews having to leave Nazi Germany," May said. "We used to know some Jewish refugees during the war – my husband used to play chess with Reuben. What a terrible time they had." "Yes, I suppose it's something like that," the woman said quietly. "Sometimes these things are so sad, aren't they – you and your daughter, me and my mother."

May finished her tea, which was much too sweet for her taste. "Shall I call the doctor for you?" "No, I think I'd like to go home now. I'll see how I feel then. Can you call a taxi for me please?" The woman took the tea things to the kitchen and rang for a taxi. May lay back in the chair. But then she remembered the parcel. "Please," she called out, "can you send the parcel for me?" The woman walked in from the kitchen. "Of course I will." May began fumbling in her bag for her purse. "No, no," said the woman, "you can pay me when I see you next. Please don't worry." "Thank you so much. Tell me, what is your name? You've been so kind, I don't know how to thank you." "My name is Mrs Khan, Fazila Khan. And you are welcome. I hope you recover soon and we will see you again."

As May stepped into the taxi, she decided that she must send a thank-you notelet to Mrs Khan – she had some nice ones at home.

The Sewing Circles

Byron Beynon

A suture on the wounds of landscape;
in Herat, under an Afghan sky

peace was lost as women
drawn together like busy thread

carried embroidered cases,
defiant covers for the words

they'd interweave against
the Taliban sentence of death.

Standing together, shedding burkas,
binding their language whole,

those improvised needles
kept sharp for the healing purl.

Pay the Price

Ian Brown

PRIME MINISTER:	... and now, conference, I turn to asylum. We have a long heritage of welcoming those who are genuinely in need of our protection and this must continue. (APPLAUSE)
ASYLUM SEEKER:	I thought we were in Canada because I'd heard them talking about Canada. We were so tired when we arrived that we went to sleep in the airport.
PRIME MINISTER:	But the nature and volume of asylum claims have changed.
IMMIGRATION:	Wake up! Refugees? Speak English?
ASYLUM SEEKER:	Yes.
IMMIGRATION:	Where are you from?
ASYLUM SEEKER:	******
PRIME MINISTER:	Significant numbers of economic migrants arrive in the UK, pretending to be from a different country.
IMMIGRATION:	Liar! You're from South Africa. People in ****** can't speak English. Take your shoes off, bitch. (TO A GROUP OF PEOPLE STANDING NEARBY) We're going to tie them up and send them back in the luggage compartment.
PRIME MINISTER:	They invent stories of persecution.
ASYLUM SEEKER:	Soldiers killed my father, my mother, my brother. My father had been a government minister after independence. We heard the shots. They came to tell us to go and get the bodies. It was

59

	terrible. Bullets, everywhere. Blood, everywhere.
IMMIGRATION:	Take your shoes off, bitch.
ASYLUM SEEKER:	The soldiers came back, three or four of them, and beat my husband with rifle butts. They took him away. My children were hiding under the bed. They asked where Daddy was. I couldn't tell them. The soldiers came back. I begged them. They talked about my father. They told me I had to pay the price.
PRIME MINISTER:	And by doing so, they were undermining the integrity of our asylum system ...
ASYLUM SEEKER:	The soldiers did many things to me in front of the children. (PAUSE) Difficult situation. Difficult to talk about.
JUDGE:	Hang on a minute. There's a discrepancy in the evidence. In the medical report you claim that four men raped you. However, the psychiatric report alleges you were raped by more than two men. (HE PUSHES HIS GLASSES DOWN TO THE TIP OF HIS NOSE) Was it seventy-six men, twenty-six men, four men? Surely you remember how many men raped you?!
PRIME MINISTER:	... and they make life harder for genuine refugees who really need our help.
JUDGE:	Appeal refused!
ASYLUM SEEKER:	I was pregnant afterwards, but I couldn't bring myself to have an abortion. We had to leave everything

and go to live with a priest. A man came to see us. He told me he could help us to leave the country, but he wouldn't allow me to take my baby because she could cause problems.

PRIME MINISTER: They destroy their documentation when they arrive and then try to claim asylum.

ASYLUM SEEKER: Sacrifice one to save four.

PRIME MINISTER: But we are clamping down on those who abuse the system. (LOUD APPLAUSE)

ASYLUM SEEKER: After I arrived here I found out I was HIV positive.

JUDGE: They can treat you back home. You look healthy enough. You're not dying!

IMMIGRATION: Even if we have to take you in a wooden box, you'll be leaving the country.

PRIME MINISTER: We have tightened the rules on benefit.

ASYLUM SEEKER: I have nightmares where I'm being chased by soldiers and they touch me and I wake up.

PRIME MINISTER: We have introduced much tougher controls on legal aid.

ASYLUM SEEKER: The worst thing is the pain I feel for my daughter. I feel I've neglected her. Abandoned her.

PRIME MINISTER: We've stepped up enforcement to tackle illegal working.

ASYLUM SEEKER: I just want to work. I'm a professional woman. Give me the opportunity to work and I'll be independent. I want to contribute to this country.

PRIME MINISTER: And our new legislation on asylum will tighten up further still, overhauling the appeals system which allowed unfounded applicants to play the system for months on end at enormous cost to the British tax payer.

ASYLUM SEEKER: I'm not a terrorist. I haven't done anything wrong in this country. My children are doing well at school. They get good reports. What else do you want?

PRIME MINISTER: We will redouble efforts to remove those who remain in this country when their applications have failed.

ASYLUM SEEKER: They're going to send people back home. If they're killed, who's responsible for the killing? (PAUSE) How can I go back? I can't go back. Never.

PRIME MINISTER: But we will always welcome lawful migrants to this country and – let me be clear, conference – we will never play politics with the issue of asylum. (STANDING OVATION)

Women in Algeria and the World

Narriman Guémar

In French, human rights are called "the Rights of Man". They are not respected in Algeria – but the rights of women are respected even less.

The legal code which governs family life, the "Family Code", dictates how women live their lives in a totally discriminatory fashion. Women in Algeria are not free at any age to give their own consent to marriage, but must be spoken for by a male *tuteur* or guardian. They cannot obtain a divorce except under stringent conditions. The father enjoys sole authority (*tutelage*) over the children. In theory, polygamy is outlawed, but in practice, women cannot prevent their husbands from taking other wives.

Girls are much less likely to receive an education than boys, and many older women are illiterate. Women workers are far more vulnerable to dismissal than men. As a matter of fact, working women are mostly unmarried women. Article 39 of the Family Code imposes on women the duty to obey their husbands, which means that a man can forbid his wife to take a job, or indeed engage in any other activity against his wishes.

Many women are victims of violence, mostly in their own homes, the abuser usually being the father, husband, brother, or perhaps an uncle or brother-in-law. Half of all rapes are committed upon minors, and many are incestuous. Abortion is illegal, so as a result there are very high numbers of single unmarried mothers and abandoned children.

Other forms of violence have become commonplace since some women began to become educated and participate in public life and in the job market. Women living alone often face unremitting aggression from men around them. But sexual harassment is a taboo topic. Complaints are very rare.

Women in distress as a result of such pressures have nowhere to turn for support. There is also a glaring lack of provision for women victims of terrorism. Despite an official discourse of solidarity and compassion for women raped by terrorist groups, absolutely no structures have been put in place by the State to offer real, practical help.

Another issue concerns the wives of the 'disappeared' of the so-called 'terrorist decade', the 1990s. Thousands of women have suffered the disappearance of a husband whose fate remains unknown to this very day, and many of them endure extreme hardship and poverty. A friend of mine – a fellow union activist – found that she was unable to obtain a death certificate. But without one, she could neither exercise legal authority over her child nor have access to any inheritance. Refused the status of widow or even of divorcee, she had to fight for many years for her elementary rights to be recognised.

These issues affecting Algerian women have to be seen in a wider context, that of the global economy and politics. It is often said that globalisation offers opportunities for women, especially in poor countries: opportunities to enter the job market and hence emancipate themselves and escape misery. But the statistics show the opposite: around the world, women, 50% of the population, do two thirds of the total hours worked (both paid and domestic). Yet women earn only one tenth of world income, and they own only 1% of world wealth. Of the 1.3 billion people currently living below the level of absolute poverty, 70% are women.

Far from improving women's position, the effects of capitalist globalisation weigh heavily on them and are making them more and more vulnerable. When women enter the world of paid work they mostly endure harsh extremes of insecurity, unprotected by any legislation, in sectors known as 'feminine', i.e. requiring the fewest qualifications and receiving the lowest pay. Often they have to take several jobs, even while they continue to be responsible for all the household labour. The dismantling of public services demanded by the policies of the IMF in countries of the South (such as Algeria), or the austerity policies demanded in the North (such as the UK), have serious consequences for women. When schooling has to be paid for, girls are less likely to get an elementary education. In the Third World, two women in three cannot read or write. Access to medical services is also often blocked when these are privatised.

To bring about a real improvement in women's lives, a struggle has to be fought on two fronts: both against capitalist globalisation and against patriarchy, the domination of men. It is patriarchy which provides the ideological justification for women being paid less than men for the same work, or for women being expected to do all unpaid household labour. Let all of us, women and men, fight together to cancel Third World debt, to provide secure employment for all, to bring about real equality between men and women in the workplace, but also in the home, and to provide automatic access to contraception! Let us all demand a world without exploitation, where women and men will be equal!

Monika

Hamira A. Geedy

Like my other published stories, this one is a true story, but for some details. It happened to one of my patients when I was working as a GP in Iran.

"I am sorry, madam, but this one small procedure needs to be performed, and I cannot be sure what will happen to her hymen during the course of the operation ..."

She remembers the doctor's words from when she was a little girl, but nobody in the family ever spoke about it afterwards. Now Monika, at 17, is a grown woman, with good looks, a big attractive smile, sexy-looking long dark curly hair. She's loved by Manochehr, strong and romantic, from a smart family, who tells his mother: "I don't care, even if I could marry into the royal family! Monika's the most beautiful girl in this town, and she and I are going to get engaged!"

"So what is this secret you have, my gorgeous?" he asks her after their engagement, when she decides that she must tell him what worries her. What she then says destroys the whole world. Manochehr wouldn't ever marry someone who was "not a virgin". And everyone believes the dreadful stories that he and his mother spread.

I examined Monika five years later and told her that she was a perfectly normal virgin.

"I'm going to marry Ahmad, he's an engineer, he's 45, but he's the only one who'll accept me. I'll be able to support my mum. He's better than nothing."

He made her flesh creep, but she had nobody to rely on and an ageing mother. She said to herself:

"The die is cast."

Ten years later with two small boys, she sometimes sees her mother on the street:

"Why are you still with that dirty piece of work. Leave him!"

"How can I, what will happen to the children?"

"Get a divorce, I can look after the children, you can get a job."

"He won't let me have the children. They'd be in danger from him. He hits them so hard sometimes. I have to stand between to stop them getting hurt."

"I worry for all of you."

"I threw myself to the wolf when I married him."

She went to the police station after one beating. They told her that if she left her husband, she couldn't take her children, because she didn't have a job.

But one day when they fought he screamed: "I hate you and I hate your children!" And he threw them all out, telling her to take the children and go to her mother, and he went to court to get a divorce the next day. The settlement left her with nothing from the marriage, except, luckily, the children.

Her mother's house had few facilities and was small for all of them, but there was calm and silence. Monika found work at a hairdresser's. She spoke on the telephone with her brother, who had been accepted as a refugee in Canada after taking to the mountains with the Kurdish freedom fighters some years before. She should try to come and join him, he said.

"I can't leave mum alone. She's so feeble now."

After a while, Ahmad got the court's permission to see the children whenever he wanted. He soon lost control: "Don't lie to me. Your mother's a lying bitch, that's why I divorced her!

"No! You've got no right to insult her!"

With a flying kick, Ahmad caught Farhad in the chest and crashed him into the wall behind. Farhad's head banged against the wall and he collapsed, losing consciousness for a short while. His younger brother Farzad rushed to him. Ahmad bundled the two of them out, pulling them by their clothes and hair, screaming: "Get out, go to your bloody mother, I don't want you!"

The next time he tried to pick them up from school, they wouldn't go with him. Ahmad went to the court and was given permission. Nobody listened to Monika, and the children started to refuse to go to school.

Now her brother's suggestion was too tempting. Her mother needed constant help, but Ahmad's mistreatment of the children was too frightening. She took the children and flew to Turkey to request a visa from the UN there. While her application was processed, she was advised to register with the police in the city of Van, in the Kurdish part of Turkey. She rented a small flat and stayed there, waiting. There were more than a dozen Iranian refugee families there, with various kinds of problems, mostly political. In a foreign country, with no money and no relatives, life was hard. But at least there was nobody to threaten her and her children. She waited and hoped to get her UN visa. They all tried to learn English to prepare for a new life in Canada. She was not despondent. She worried about her mother, but she had said: "Don't worry about me. I'm the last dried yellow leaf on the dried branch of a tree in autumn, but your children are the root of the tree. Take care that this tree-root does not dry out."

"Watch out," her mother said to her one day on the phone: "Ahmad is saying he wants revenge. He says he's going to track you down and bring the children back here."

Monika visited the UN office in Ankara, only to be told:

"I'm sorry, lady. We can try to speed up your application, but there are rules we all have to work by. We can't do any more than that. You just have to wait."

After lying low for a while, hardly leaving the house, Monika heard that Ahmad had spent some time looking for them in Van but had given up and gone back to Iran. She was still cautious.

"Can we go out to the park today and play with the other children?" asked Farzad.

"No you can't!" she said automatically.

Three weeks later her mother phoned to say that her ex-husband was on his way again. Again Monika went to Ankara. Again she visited the police to ask to be moved somewhere away from Van. What did the police care about a few Kurds?

Ahmad came to the road with the small houses where the refugee families lived. Children were playing in the street.

"Hi kids! I'm Farhad and Farzad's dad. Can you help me find them?"

The children looked at him suspiciously.

"I've got presents for you, look! Mobile phones!"

Handing out these gifts from a plastic bag, Ahmad easily got the address he wanted, just round the corner.

"Hi boys, it's me! Hello Farhad, Farzad! Why are you looking at me like a stranger? Come on!"

He stood with arms wide open waiting for them.

"Come on, let me give you a hug!"

Farhad took a hesitant step forward, giving his younger brother Farzad a reassuring look. Ahmad dropped his arms and reached for the plastic bag.

"Look here! I brought you both mobile phones."

Their eyes sparkled. It was the first present their father had given them for many years.

"I've got a present for your mum, too. I know you're all going to Canada, so I won't see her again. I want her to forgive me. Stay here till I speak to your mother."

Monika was tidying the wardrobe.

"Hello my queen, so this is your new castle?"

Shocked, she spun round with a little squeak, clutching the wardrobe door.

"Finally gotcha!"

Pale and faint, hardly able to breathe, trying to seem stronger than she felt, she asked:

"What do you want?"

Trembling, she pressed against the wardrobe. Ahmad growled:

"I don't want you. Not any more. You're going to Canada, I heard, so I brought you a gift."

He reached into the plastic bag.

"I don't need any gift from you," said Monika, turning her back on him and pretending to look for something inside the wardrobe. "Why don't you just leave and forget all about us, please."

Ahmad stepped up, jerked the knife from the bag and stabbed it into Monika's shoulder with his full force. She fell half into the wardrobe, her screams muffled as he stabbed her again and again, even after she had fallen silent, and the blood dripped from the wardrobe, until he leaned against the wall, exhausted, and sagged down to the floor, his face and hands and clothes full of blood, the knife still in his hands, gasping as if he had done a heavy job.

Ahmad was jailed in Turkey. Monika's corpse was brought back to Iran. A month after her death, the visa was issued. Her children were taken to Canada, where they now live as refugees, without the love of their mother or their father.

Answer to a Question

Sylvie Hoffmann

"Why are you here? After all, there's no war in your country ...?"

Je te ferai grimper aux murs!
I'll make you crawl up the walls!
  The belt hissed.
  Blood and semen flowed out
  over the potatoes waiting to be washed and peeled –
    I saw
    my mother's face smashed in.

Tu vas m'obéir au doigt et à l'oeil!
You must obey me at the batting of my eyelid!
  The belt hissed.
  Blood and semen flowed out
  and stuck in the cracks between the tiles
                        on the scrubbed floor –
      I saw
      my eldest sister weeping.

Guili, guili, elle va être zentille la p'tite fille!
Tickle, tickle, who's going to be a good girl then!
  Uncoiled, the belt slithered.
  Blood and semen flowed out
  on the night-dress of the sick child, where it dried
                        as stiff as starch –
      I know
      she ingested her howl.

"Voilà! Now you know! May I still stay, or does it not count?"

Know Your Strangers?

Maxson Sahr Kpakio

In this new environment, some of the welcome ceremonies are so different that strangers are always in fear of being met by certain so-called locals.

I remember after just about eight months as a stranger arriving in my new home, looking for a place I will no longer hear the sound of guns, looking for a place I will no longer see people being shot and killed right before my eyes, looking for a place I will no longer jump over dead bodies in search of food, looking for a place I will have relative peace of mind, I came across a certain local who rushed before my eyes and shouted: "Go home where you come from, this is not your country."

Now, two and half years later, a physical attack has caused me some hours in the hospital. This attack was indeed racially motivated.

From my childhood days growing up in a little West African country, one important thing I always remember is the way strangers are so much respected, welcomed, and cared for by the local citizens. In my youth, I travelled across some of my country's close neighbours, including the very British colonies, Sierra Leone, Ghana and Nigeria. In these countries as in my country, we welcome strangers in a good and friendly manner. As a stranger, even if a person cannot help or provide for your needs in any way, the good thing is that you will find someone who will befriend you and smile with you.

But little did I know that this kind of welcome is not everywhere, until I arrived in my new horizon.

Early one morning recently a friend sent me a text: Hi, how about this title for our next book: "Know Your Strangers"? I thought to write some piece that will go along with this title. Three days later, while putting my ideas together, I was racially attacked, openly assaulted in broad daylight on Swansea High Street.

Is this is how strangers should be known? By attacking them verbally and telling them to go back where they come from? By hitting them on the back of their neck and taking their life away? By assaulting them simply because of their race? By abusing them and chanting racist chants? By dashing their change into their hands, looking away? By refusing to recognise them as human beings?

This is truly what we as strangers least expected.

If you can't help, don't hurt ...

Hoshyar: Awake

Tom Cheesman

Saddam's survivor chilled
with some of his mates
and some Swansea Jills
out late.

Because the sight filled
a passer-by with hate
Saddam's survivor was killed
in the street.

Saddam lives to be tried
for genocide.

Hoshyar lies in Iraq.

Mordecai sent him back
never to awake.

In Memoriam Kalan Kawa Karim

Jeni Williams

A fine day for the march. The curious
watched from doorways then walked off to unknown
busy lives, bored with chant and furious
protest. But, by the roadside and alone

for the quiet minute's length, an old man
slowly uncovered his head. He looked down,
acknowledging the brief and shattered span
of a good life, then left. No speech in town

denouncing such purposeless violence,
moved me so much as that man standing there,
head bent, holding his cap, the small silence
growing all round us. We walked to the square

and the cars, which had paused for the event,
moved on into a new, sunlit moment.

Give Me Your Hand Kalan Kawa Karim

Richard Jones

Give me your hand Kalan Kawa Karim:
Unfamiliar with my wasted land,
Not seeing the pools of sickness around you,
You dream of mountainous horizons

To be climbed slowly, ignoring the pains
That nag every step on the way back home.
They call this road The Kingsway. You ask why
There are no monuments to their greatness,

Being used to statues in any open square,
His face everywhere you dare to raise your eyes,
The penetrating stare that reached where
None could hear your desperate futile cries.

You smile. The last time you saw him he looked
Like that tea-cosy tramp in the garden.
His slack jaw gaped helpless for all to see.
Even a tramp showed greater dignity

Than this fallen torturer. Your heart leapt
Knowing the return journey could begin.
Take the first steps then, past The Potter's Wheel,
Feel your face fresh in the breath of sea wind.

Give me your hand Kalan Kawa Karim:
There is yet one more dark night to cross
And though all the time here they sing of welcomes,
Still fear strikes down the man who dares to dream.

Never Forget Halabja

Kamaran Najmadin

In the town of Halabja on the Bloody Friday of the 17th of March 1988 the Iraqi regime killed over five thousand Kurdish people and wounded over seven thousand more.

It was just a few days before the Kurdish people celebrate Newroz, their New Year festival.

Halabja was attacked more than twenty times by warplanes with chemical and cluster bombs.

Now, after everything Saddam Hussein did with the Kurdish people, he is in jail, and the Kurdish leader Jalal Talabani has become the new president of Iraq.

Now everybody in Iraq is feeling happy. But nobody can forget that Bloody Friday. It was horrible.

It still is. Isn't it?

The Bridge of the God Daabhawor

Showan Khurshid

It is usually said that human sacrifice is performed for religious reasons. But Billaru, the capital city of the Kiran Empire, located on the river Euphrates, somewhere not far south of the modern city of Baghdad, was different. Six millennia ago, the wise men here – witnessing how power struggles destroy life, civilisation, even decency, pitting son against father, brother against brother – concluded that nothing mattered more than political stability. They suspected that political rivalry was the problem. They did not know democracy, which manages political rivalry by means of rights and elections. Instead, they thought that they might be able to prevent political rivalry through human sacrifice.

The wise men did not spell out their reasoning, perhaps thinking that it would not convince the common people. They framed their justification in religious language. However, as always, people design things but things acquire lives of their own. Let me report my vision to you.

Nebon Terrat stands on the bridge, tears into small pieces a letter written on a leaf of papyrus, throws the pieces into the river Euphrates and says in resignation: "It is over." The executioner Tinal Tinal, about fifty years old, big and powerfully built, asks in a tone of equal resignation and sadness: "Are you ready?" Nebon Terrat, a prince, the brother of the king, thirteen years old, has been chosen to be the human sacrifice of this season, and he answers "Yes," as if nothing concerns him.

The bridge where the young prince and the executioner are standing is narrow and short. It is called the Bridge of the

God Daabhawor because his temple has been built there. The temple looks like two hands, one on each side of the bridge. These hands burst out, up through the crust of the earth at the top of the hill, tense, reflecting a violent act of catching someone or something and burying the object in the underworld of horror.

The river beneath the bridge is narrow and deeper here than elsewhere. Hills are rare in this area. Rivers and streams naturally tend to circumvent them, or eventually sweep them away. But here the river passes right through the hill, slicing it from top to bottom. The river bed is narrow, so the water builds up pressure, spurting in speeding currents, producing whirlpools here and there on either side of the bridge. Unsurprisingly, swimming is very risky here. I am told, in fact, that of every ten swimmers who dare to enter the water, three drown and another three are mentally or physically crippled.

Even the mere act of walking on the bridge is very dangerous, and no wonder: it is only about one and a half meters wide and very high over the water. There is no handrail, so the slightest dizziness or a brisk breeze or an attack of vertigo suffices to throw pedestrians onto the rocky sides of the chasm or into the mouth of the whirlpools. In fact, all the priests of the temple are young, and not because the older ones, being sensible and aware of the risk, have retired – retirement is forbidden. Rather, it is because most of the priests have fallen into the river on the first occasion of nausea, the first stiff breeze or a panic due to vertigo.

In the middle of the bridge is a circular area, wider than the rest of the bridge, and in the centre of this circle is a circular hole. The hole is constructed such that the human sacrifice can be made to kneel at the edge of it, bowing forward, stretching his neck, and when his head is chopped off by a single lightning-fast blow, it will fall through the hole and down into the river below.

The ritual of human sacrifice does not end there. The head is supposed to be retrieved and put on display in the main square of the city for three weeks. The ceremony is thus designed to be as difficult and deadly as possible. The formal religious explanation for its necessity runs as follows: "We have a bargain with the god Daabhawor. We give him our most beloved, most beautiful, most intelligent and most innocent head. We let him taste it, but we recover it immediately. This way, he respects us and helps us maintain stability in our country. If we fail to recover the head, he gives us another chance, then a third one and so on. The sacrifices only end when we succeed in recovering a head."

But who would dare to swim beneath that bridge where three out of every ten daring swimmers are drowned and three others crippled? The authorities could not fail to be aware of this dilemma. They were very creative in their own way. They must have assumed that people, particularly political rivals, might not be deterred by a single killing of an innocent boy in an empire of a million or so, especially when this sacrifice is a member of the royal family and thus a potential asset to the rulers. They may have suspected that potential rivals would only be delighted. They reasoned that the task of deterrence and subjugation requires the elimination of a few hundred at least, and it must be the bereaved kings who choose these further victims. Therefore, after the sacrifice, other ceremonial killings, though less grandiose ones, must begin. Being aware of this, those who suspected that they might be on the king's death-list would come forward to seek mercy or to offer their dearest ones to be killed in their stead. Self-denouncing opponents of the king or of the system would come forward in their thousands. Many could be forgiven. But others would be offered a deal: take the risk of swimming beneath the bridge and collecting the head, and if they were among the lucky survivors, they would have a greater chance of being forgiven.

And the one who succeeds in recovering a head would be granted the right to chop off the head of a member of his own caste, anyone he chooses, without being asked to justify his choice or to declare whether he hates or loves that person.

Being spared this question is no trivial matter. Indeed it is a great privilege, because loving in this city is a very big issue. Here, when you love someone, you are supposed to offer to sacrifice him or her, or else yourself – though only, of course, after seeking the authorities' permission. The idea behind this has already been implied. It is that you shouldn't love anybody, because if you do, you might start doing what they would like you to do, and so you might even revolt against the authorities, for example if your beloved told you to, or if you thought that you could impress them by doing so. But in fact, people can't stop loving. Hence the people of Bilaru become very distressed about the possibility of being interrogated as to whether they love somebody or not. Of course this is very unnatural, but nevertheless, they are told that this is the most rational choice for the population of the Kiran empire. In religious courses and rituals, they are told numerous stories about the terrible things that have happened or are happening to people who do otherwise. Indeed, not all of these stories are fabricated.

But again, people can't stop loving. Instead, they have developed a whole culture to cope with and disguise loving. One of the methods of coping with loving, when you know you won't be strong enough to suppress your affection, is to smuggle out any loved ones. People smuggle their sons, daughters, girlfriends, brothers, even mothers and fathers out into the outlying plains and marshlands or far away to the mountains to the north and north-east.

But there are other disturbing and sometimes very absurd consequences of this situation. One sees people who, in order to disguise their affection, act as if they hated their loved ones. In public, they fabricate some excuse to blame their loved one, affect anger and begin mistreating them. Sometimes, anxiety overtakes them that their mistreatment may not look genuine enough: they beat the loved one to death without realising it.

In strange conditions, people become strange. Some try to take advantage of the system. A person who hates another very much, instead of expressing that hatred, shows affection, in the hope that their enemy will be chosen as a human sacrifice. So when two people fight, one will declare at the top of his voice: "You know what? I think it's about time I told you the truth. I can't go on pretending that I hate you. I love you. Enough is enough. I'm a human being, I can't hide my affection for you any more." And he begins crying and sobbing and then says: "Forgive me, my love, I failed you!" The other says: "No, please be honest. I don't need your love. Until now we were a couple of decent enemies." The first says: "But I can't help it, I love you!" and he shouts out: "You people, hear me! I have sinned and I love this man!" The second says: "He is lying!" in a very ceremonial way which is expected on such occasions.

In the beginning, many centuries earlier, when these measures were first introduced, people had not developed all the potential coping strategies. Some tried making counter-allegations: "No, no, on the contrary, it's me who loves him and not the other way around!" This was because they were hoping that the other would be sent to die instead. But this proved to be both futile and deadly, because the authorities would say: "Well, it seems that you both love each other greatly. And as you are both exemplary citizens, and we have no reason to suspect the integrity of either of you, we'll put you both to death." That is why the Kiran people, nowadays, try other ways, which offer a better chance of survival and perhaps some unexpected advantages as well. When they quarrel and one of them reports the other to the authorities, the latter will say, ceremoniously again: "Well, this is a very grave matter. But I demand the right for love confinement."

Love confinement is another brilliant invention of the Kiran. This is not what one might expect, i.e. two lovers going on something like a honeymoon, confining themselves so that nothing distracts them from their complete mutual devotion. Rather, it is another peculiarity of the Kiran empire. The rationale of this institution goes like this. When a person loves another, they may do anything to appease or impress the beloved. This implies real danger to the system, because they may rebel. Therefore, both should be put in prison for a limited time, to ensure that the system is safe from them. The prescribed period is four months.

Why only four months? Because a longer period would be very expensive for the authorities. In the beginning of the institution of love confinement, the period was just two months. But many who were concerned with justice thought that two months was not long enough. They petitioned the king to extend the period. The matter became, in fact, a big rallying issue. The poor and the middle classes, led by lower and middle ranking priests, backed the proposal and argued that the king should tax the rich and extend the love confinement period to four months, at least. Successive kings promised and procrastinated and there was a secret prayer in every temple that the wishes of the people might be granted. It seemed that reform would require a long and bloody struggle. But the will of the people always prevails, as you know. At last the current king's late father granted the extension. There was real celebration. He became very popular, though of course nobody said that they loved the king. His popularity spilled over to his son, the current king, as well. Now almost everyone feels that four months is very fair. When two persons are to be taken to love confinement, a priest (who usually has two or three fingers missing on each hand) comes and says: "Our generous system will give you four months of seclusion during which you have to prove which one of you is honest."

This is the secret of the priests with missing fingers: during the Struggle for Four Months of Love Confinement, the sign by which proponents identified themselves became the flashing of four fingers. When the authorities noticed this, they began chopping off two fingers so that people would not be able to make this sign. Sometimes they chopped off three fingers, in order to remind people that "two is the number."

In love confinement, the alleged lover must endure everything done to him by the alleged loved one, which may include all kinds of physical and psychological abuse, humiliation and torture. But the alleged lover must express great happiness and gratitude, on the theory that you can't love someone unless you presume, deep down, that he or she is good – and a good person does good things to you. Because the citizens are expected to prove their integrity during the confinement, no one may go so far as killing the other. Nevertheless, the alleged lover endures something not much less horrible than a nightmarish death. In the end of this period, if the alleged lover has endured, he is released and the other is put to death. But if he recants, he receives a short prison sentence – a few weeks or even just a few days. The authorities reasoned, rightly it seems, that no one who can endure the most horrible enslavement, if only for a short period, will regain a self capable of posing any political threat. In fact, such people, on being released, usually go and voluntarily become the slave of someone they happened to hate or love (of course, you would not know for sure which feeling it was). And those who succumb before the period of love confinement is up become the slave of their former enemy.

There are other advantages for the alleged beloved. They acquire the bearing and demeanour of a master. Some go on to organise courses on the techniques of "Beating False Love and Enduring Love Confinement." But even some alleged lovers, having endured beating and humiliation, offer courses: "How to Endure the Torture of the Beloved Successfully and Send Him to His Death." These educators are held in high esteem and are indeed celebrities in Billaru.

This situation makes it very hard to find out who loves whom or who hates whom, or even what love is. As a result, when you see someone about to swim in the river, you may suspect that that person's chosen victim will be you. Thus, if you are somehow conspicuous and have the slightest hope that you may survive, you too will enter the river. Not necessarily because you hate someone and want his head chopped off. It is only in order to be able to choose rather than be chosen.

Such mechanisms of recruitment swell the number of swimmers to many hundreds. Of course, outsiders are not told what is going on, only that it is a matter of religious devotion. Everyone around behaves as if they are very pious. And because of this, strangers to the city are immensely impressed by the great faith of these people.

So now we know: there are plenty of people waiting afloat under the bridge. Some are drowning or having their brains starved of oxygen to suffer permanent mental or physical handicap later. These people in the river, as we know, are supposed to retrieve the heads, but the authorities, being obsessed with rationalisation, assigned them yet another task: "Since you are there anyway," they declared, "you can catch the sacrifice if he happens to jump into the water."

Above the bridge, as we know, are Tinal Tinal and the Prince Nebon Terrat, both resigned to giving themselves passively to the process of the ritual. When the boy answered: "Yes," Tinal told him: "Go to the edge of the circular hole to kneel there, bow forward and stretch your neck," so that he could cut his head off as easily and painlessly as possible. Nebon Terrat did as he was told and kneeled, but he didn't bow forward. Without looking at Tinal Tinal, as if indifferently, he said: "Before I bow forward and extend my neck, I'd like to look around and reflect a little bit. Kill me any time you want, if you feel impatient." Nebon Terrat began looking around.

The bridge is short, so he can clearly see the faces of the people waiting on the hill, a few of them unable to conceal their excitement. People are used to seeing death in every aspect of their lives and conditioned to regard it as a necessity for stability. Dying is considered as a purifying process. However, being unable to choose the one who is to die, they take some comfort from this deprivation by watching someone else die. This is really equivalent to the way we look at boxing. We would like to punch our adversaries but we can't, so we seek compensation by watching someone else being punched, and we always identify with the winner and reward him as if we were rewarding ourselves after a great effort at beating all our bastard enemies. The Romans' gladiators offered much the same kind of purifying spectacle.

However, there is an important difference between the ritual on the bridge and boxing or gladiators. We reveal our excitement and pleasure at having our 'adversaries' beaten and humiliated. But the display of such emotions was not considered appropriate in this religious setting. So it is not easy to see the real mood on most of the spectators' faces. Nevertheless, the excitement is seeping out in many different ways. It even infects Terrat Terrat, the king. Some of the public and priests, in order to paint over their emotions, are chanting: "Great, great is Daabhawor, great, great is Daabhawor." Nebon Terrat looks over to where his brother Terrat Terrat is standing. The king is watching him with an expression of impatience, excitement and anticipation.

It seems that the king has relaxed his guard because he does not need to be worried about others seeing his face, since he is in the front row. Nebon Terrat starts wondering if it is true that the king loves him as he has said he does; maybe he just wants to get rid of him?

He suspects his brother. He has heard that he is not childless, as is officially claimed. Rather, he has a son who was smuggled out. This is a plausible rumour because he himself, until the last few weeks, was a sent-away son of the late king. So he thinks: "If my father was cheating on the system, why wouldn't my brother?" His suspicion grows stronger as he reflects that in fact the king is only his half-brother. Now he is wondering: "Probably the king has brought me back to be sacrificed instead of his own son, in order to secure the succession for him." He and his brother have never lived together, apart from the last few weeks, so how come his brother suddenly loves him, and worse, announces his love?

These thoughts and the excited face of his brother shatter his earlier resignation and peace of mind. I hear him telling the executioner: "I'm not afraid of dying, but it is senseless to die for these ridiculous beliefs, this bloody god, this stupid system and amongst these stupid faces. You may kill me now. I'd rather you stabbed me in the heart."

What did he say? He's insulting the god, the people and the regime! I expect this to enrage the executioner, who will chop him into pieces before he finishes him off. But this is not happening. Meanwhile I'm asking myself, why would he be blaspheming like this?

People are rarely disappointed by their religions. Instead they are disappointed by their leaders or priests. Hence my surprise at Nebbon Terrat's blasphemy. I was not expecting the prince to get angry about the religion. I expected him to shout out at the top of his voice, cursing his brother the king because he is not sacrificing his own son, whom he presumably loves more. However, I realise now that something different is going on. Nebbon Terrat's angry exclamation about "these ridiculous beliefs, this bloody god, this stupid system and amongst these stupid faces" is not just a reaction to the injustice which is about to befall him. Rather, these words reflect his upbringing in the mountains where, in the absence of a highly centralised political system, people have a very relaxed attitude to religions and gods, and although they live under harsh conditions, take issues of belief light-heartedly. They cannot understand that a religion should stipulate such a stupid thing as the killing of the best beloved.

Yet another expectation of mine is violated. If Nebon Terrat's background could explain why he is different, what about Tinal Tinal? I expected the young prince's sacrilegious expressions to throw Tinal Tinal into a fit of rage. A Billaruian in his position should surely at least have gone to the highest priest and told him what the sacrifice had said. The priests would have declared the sacrifice rebellious, which would have made him highly valuable for Daabhawor, and they would have sent for two other people to tie him down and prepare his neck for the chop. But Tinal Tinal is not really a Billaruian. He is from somewhere further to the west in the bush region which is desert now. He used to live independently and happily with his family. One day, he came back from hunting to find that some robbers had raided his home and killed his son, who, just like Nebon Terrat, was only thirteen years old. The boy had bravely confronted them and foiled the attempted robbery. They had run away, but in a hateful rage caused by their humiliation at the hands of what they regarded as a mere child, they had come back and killed him with a poisoned arrow. Tinal Tinal swore then that he would henceforth have only one purpose in life, namely to track down criminals and let them feel the death which they dispensed to other people. As such, he actually functioned, machine-like, as a one-man justice system. But later he realised that some people had taken advantage of him and used him to hunt down and kill innocent people. This happened to him, I assume, because no matter how much you try to act in good faith, you just cannot be a self-contained justice system all on your own.

Realising that he had victimised innocents in the pursuit of justice, Tinal Tinal cursed all people. He decided that only a very heavy-handed, colossal system that denies all desires and passions and puts fear in every heart can control corrupt human nature. "Remember Hobbes," I was told in my vision. "He wanted no less than a Leviathan."

This was Tinal Tinal's mood when he met some people from Billaru. Although some of them were dissidents and had fled the system to the wilderness, they spoke quite positively about their religion. This raises an interesting question: Why should somebody flee a cruel political system, only to go around promoting the very belief system which underlies the political system which victimised and exiled him? But this happens even now. After all, the belief system of Billaru was presented to the people as good, and they certainly took pride in it. They put the blame for what they found horrible in the system – not the prohibition of love or the practice of human sacrifice, but rather the cheating which was prevalent – on their leaders. To blame the leaders is easier than blaming the system of belief. If you blame the belief, you also lose your people, and even if you flee you will not become a part of a new group, you will remain a foreigner for ever. This is why most people keep their old beliefs.

The dissidents of Bilaru, like all Bilaruians, chanted thousands of times over: "Dary dary Daabhawor daras," meaning: "Great, great is the Greatest Daabhawor." This must have brain-washed them. No wonder they felt overwhelmed by his greatness. The more they chanted, the more they felt overwhelmed. Brain-washed people can even feel very sorry for you, if they know that you're a good person but you don't have the same beliefs as they do. They come and try to convert you. It is like Muslims nowadays whose lives in their own countries become intolerable, mainly thanks to Islam itself, and who try as hard as they can to get away to other parts of the world, but once there, they entreat most passionately, preach, and exhort others to convert to Islam.

Tinal Tinal must have been a victim of such confusions, the target of appeals and proselytising campaigns. He converted to the Kiran religion and although nearly everyone told him not to go to Billaru, some did advise him to do so, and he told himself: "Let me go and see with my own eyes."

Once there, he found he was a legendary figure whose fame had reached Billaru decades before. He was assigned to execute some love sacrifices. In the beginning, given his conviction that inducing fear is all-important, he was certain of the justice of the task assigned to him. So he happily chopped off heads, one after another. He did not even mind that these heads belonged to those who were the most innocent, beautiful and lovable. In some sense he did not take such attributions literally. Being a diligent worker, he was assigned more and more heads to chop off. Eventually, the great number of heads he was chopping off alarmed him. But he did not revolt. He asked for temporary leave: some time for contemplation. "Contemplation of what?" the bosses asked themselves. They suspected him of having his own notions of right and wrong.

However, they did allow him temporary leave. Later, when it was time to execute Nebon Terrat, he was recalled and told: "You are given the honour of sending the head of the most beloved, the most beautiful, the most intelligent and the most innocent to the great god Daabhawor."

"Do you mean this literally?" Tinal Tinal asked faintly. "Of course, of course, pious believer and great hero, Tinal Tinal." "How can a human being kill the most innocent?" Tinal Tinal asked himself. "My conscience is already burdened. Do they want to drown my conscience in crime?" However, he said nothing and accepted the task, perhaps because he could not believe that they could possibly be so evil. Or he may have been developing the mentality of professionalism or careerism, where you do what you are told without taking moral responsibility. Possibly he wanted to believe that they were using the term "most innocent" in some different, special sense. Or perhaps Tinal Tinal was losing faith in human beings and was seeing no meaning in anything. Or again, he may have been feeling that he was getting old and should not take too many risks. After all, he enjoyed good facilities and even a few slaves to boot. But there was another thought that went on tormenting him: that he might have been intimidated and cowed. This last idea really upset him. "How can I be reduced to being driven by fear, and why don't they just relieve me from this particular task which I don't like when there are all these jerks out there who envy me and would happily undertake the task?"

It was against this background that Nebon Terrat's abusive mention of the god of Billaru and "this stupid system" did not upset Tinal Tinal. Instead he said: "If you're not convinced, why don't you just jump?"

Nebon Terrat answered, as if consulting a friend: "Don't you see those bastards down there? If they catch me, the authorities will make me wish I was dead."

Tinal Tinal replied: "Well my son," – but he didn't hear himself saying "my son" – "if you're armed, they won't dare come near you," and he gave him his dagger. "Good luck", he said. Nebon Terrat jumped and Tinal Tinal followed him, shouting: "I warn you, no one touches him, he's my son!"

My Presence is Here But

Maxson Sahr Kpakio

My presence is here but
My heart is in the alleyways of Monrovia
My tongue utters its name
My lips sing a song of Monrovia
The trees even the cotton trees are shrouded in inky blue
The palava hut doors never open
Matters are no longer settled in there
Years, months, weeks, days mourning Monrovia
Oh traveller! Traverse my town silently
For in the morning is Monrovia
In the evening is Monrovia
Even when it is bedtime there is Monrovia

Who is concerned?
Who is strong-hearted enough to say a word?
He who knows its streets, its places
Murmurs "Where am I?" in Monrovia
Oh God, you who are both benevolent and wrathful
Your magnificence disposes elsewhere
Your anger, your very anger is vented on Monrovia
Mother of the Lone Star undeserving of this cruelty
Undeserving of this affliction, Monrovia
Complains, shouts, screams and cries:
This was not preordained

Dark days, dark times
Sombre days, the destiny and misery of Monrovia
Day in, day out they asked: what is happening?
What is going on in the box of matches?
Only the plant of sadness
Grows in the wetland of Monrovia

Mourning is the morning of Monrovia, sorrow its night
Even the trees no longer express their colourful nature
The air is full of smells
Of poison

All adventures have a beginning and an end
An adventure without full stops is Monrovia
The lips can no longer show their colour
The tears have finally taken over
The hand of God must surely intervene
The hand of Satan
Is powerless to relieve the agony of Monrovia
The living are miserable and wretched
The sorrowless are the deceased of Monrovia
Dead before their time, without healer, without remedy
The sick children and orphans of Monrovia

It should be released from destruction
My permanence, your permanence
Is the permanence of Monrovia

At dawn, the water-seller carries his empty cow-skin
He dreams of water, the water-seller of Monrovia
From annihilation, liberate Monrovia
Let its citizens survive
If they live out all their days, so surely will Monrovia
The yellow leaves of the tall and gracious poplar
Raise up a hand praying for Monrovia

Years, months, weeks of destruction
How can this be destroyed?
From the dawn of time God was omnipresent in Monrovia
As tyrant strangers and their followers
Spill the blood of innocents
Oh God, oh God! is the cry for help

The strangers surged in, broke down
The gateways of knowledge
Shattered the windows of learning
They who are illiterate are now
The spiritual teachers of Monrovia
We are plunged into the abyss of the Stone Age
The painters of vanity have become the leaders of
Monrovia
The age slides relentlessly backwards
The advantaged are the heathens of Monrovia

In Dupoe Road, every second
The keepers of life await death
Why move about in the streets?
The lucky ones still out there turn slowly
Into particles of dust
To be carried away by natural forces
Others, the dogs take care of where they lie
For hours, for days, even for months

See the sky, but no sun
The people no longer step in where they used to
The villages are deserted
Do the people across the land really care?
Survival becomes an impossible moment
Stories have become impossible to tell in the open
Even the elders can no longer meet openly
The trees are all leafless
There were Queens yesterday
But no-one wears the crowns
Kings, but the respected robes
Are nowhere to be found

Useless, useless the life ...
It is unimaginable
No more crops
As justice lies in the hands of the strangers
They call it jungle justice
Every moment the living are silenced
That strange noise is being made by the strangers
Very fearful it is
Commandos, so-called freedom fighters
(Their self-made title)
United in undemocracy, silencing the living everlastingly
They send them to the great beyond
Its skeleton shadow on the broad-backed wave

Impossible even to find a fitting spot
To dig a loved one's grave

There is no sitting around the table
Where the darkness of barbarism hangs over the land
They talk but no-one hears them
They even scream but the feelings remain shut in
The days are numbered
Friends are now enemies
The hunt continues only by starlight
Going to bed at night becomes dangerous
Worry begins when the birds begin to sing
The morning is great, high twenties centigrade
Anarchy, the people govern themselves
Is it good for them?
The language of love is no longer among them

Day by day
Night by night
Moment by moment and minute by minute
Day by day and night by night
State of perpetual conflict
The dark cloud the order of the day
Even the believers no longer admit new members
The meeting house is sealed
But can they be blamed?
Is it willingly done?
Oh no
But no mourning can restore what once was lost
In the name of liberty
Yes, this is how it is known, even to visitors

As for the indigenous
They are betrayed by what is false within
At the age of five they witnessed it
Two years later, one by one they are consecrated
Constrained?
Even the unwilling sometimes become leaders
What a pity though, what a pity
For every moment the breeze passes by
Bitterness takes its place
The mind is no longer at peace
As it is said, even the tooth and the tongue
Misunderstand one another

The closer it gets, the more they get into themselves
In the midst of battle
It engulfed the entire breathing ground
Vision without reality
Dreams without results
Unbearable alarm sounding
The feelings of yesterday
Where is it anyway, where is it, they asked
Whenever it is remembered
Strong emotions arise and the heart becomes dark
Bleak are the hours that follow
Even the new born are hopeless and the old continue to
count the remaining hours
Celebration is no longer under the sun
They are constantly gripped by fear

Love?
Expressions are no longer on the surface
Success is no longer measured among the masses
What a pity, what a pity, what a pity

Out of Darkness (Three Poems)

Eric Ngalle Charles

Out of darkness

Out of darkness
Comes a soul and voice united
Riding through echoes of dawn
Thundering voices of apocalypse
Masked wrinkles

Through trees of swamp
Mountains of swollen hearts
They ride

Pause

Silent she walks
So she must go
Depose these garments of an outcast

With friends she sings
Lamenting the pain of Job
A poetry without name and audience

Pause

Here lies my dilemma
Between sleep and dawn

Here lies my dilemma
Flowing through Mesopotamia

Turning dreams to visions

Flowing into a sanctuary
Where the Nile meets dry land

Winter birds

The winter swans
Are coming home

They travelled west
For fair climates
From their hostile homes

This lost soul
Back with them now
Soul of the wind
Which carried them
From the land of north
To the land of west
Guided by a will to succeed

Controlled by the gods of winds
Sitting on dried leaves
Watching how others come and go

From dawn till dusk
And all my wishes confined
In a thousand cells

Each journey
My wishes' final call

O God of my ancestors

And me
Shall I heed the cuckoo's call?
And build my castle
Upon twisted hair
And my brown skin

I felt like a god (between you and me)

In the end there was this bright spring
When I broke the bridge of life and death

The sea was filled with waves of worms
Resting upon your womb
Calmed by the hands of an angel

And she was made whole
In the gaze of Cain or pain at the world
In the corners of an age crying

She cried loud
Her name Jolie
Her noise muted by milk from Debra's breast
A gift from mother to daughter
To thread this journey between you and me
Two nations

And now the random close
Between three and four
As I explain to her how mankind bleeds
Across the fields of Baghdad and the sage wisdom is slain

And of this nest Debra
That Jolie rest her head

And when the rain of night has quenched her thirsts
And your breast milk sapped the fever from her bones
And from this green world darkness ascends
O don't make me choose between these two
Heaven – Earth

I will escape the morning worms
And find solace amongst crumbling rocks

Peace

This poem was written during my final separation from Debra, my proper wife. We had issues, which from a politically correct point of view could be seen as racism. Our child Jolie was caught up in these two worlds. She ate "white man's food" from her mother and "black man's food" from me. She sings songs like "Ezruki, emuka" ("We have arrived, no we haven't arrived") and listens to music from the Riverside Festival. She speaks Russian and French with me and she says, "You speak Spanish don't you dad?" She's a three year old, "she hasn't got a clue." She doesn't know the difference between yesterday and today. She says, "Dad, I met you six years ago." I'm like, "Yes, that's because you are three," she says, "No dad, I'm four soon." She says, "I want to have big muscles like you," I say to her, "I was a slave on my mother's farm for years to develop these muscles," she says, "Don't worry dad, I'm from Ely, there's a Fitness First by the nursery." We went for her booster jabs, she thought they were muscle enhancers.

Sometimes she says, "Dad, you're not my friend anymore," but I sing to her, "Come back darling, give me another chance, I will make you satisfied" and "I never knew love between father and daughter could be so sweet."

Like many little people I know, she thinks Africa is a country. She sings songs in Welsh thanks to Miss Procter her head teacher – thirty-nine or not she shines like a rose.

I have introduced Jolie to Mr Grahame Davies my mentor, Dean Collins, Andrew Goodwin, all good friends indeed, Charlie Crowe, Gabrielle Morgan, Tom Cheesman, Sarah Newman (that I so admire!), Dr Russell Holden (head of the history department at UWIC), Dr Russell Deacon (who thought his daughter was big till he met Jolie). I would like her to be an artist and meet my friend Joanna Williams, but her mum constantly reminds me that "if horses had wishes, then riders would beg."

Swansea Collage 3

Composed by Sylvie Hoffmann

Based on conversations with asylum seekers and refugees, men, women and children from Liberia, Algeria, Zimbabwe, Iran, Morocco, Bangladesh and Congo-Kinshasa.

Lauraann's colours

"Bright yellows, to lift me up, a little bright orange to lift me up some more, a baby kind of blue, to heal, a little clear glass ... and I leave the lines and shapes to you."

Lauraann Da Costa Grobler, from Zimbabwe, died of cancer before I finished the glass panels. Her colours will be placed at the entrance to Singleton Hospital breast cancer ward.

My name is blue ...

(Group text composed by mothers and children in an Art and ESOL class at the WEA)

My name is blue and white with stripes
My name is orange and yellow with flowers
My name is cream and peach with gold
My name is a scarf with zig-zags ...

Are you happy with that?

At the solicitor's:

I'm afraid we don't have an interpreter for your language.
... Are you happy with that?
No, I'm sorry, "I'm afraid" does not mean that I am afraid.
There is nothing to fear.
... Are you happy with that?
All communications and letters will be in English.
... Are you happy with that?
No, I'm not asking you how you feel. "Are you happy with
that?" simply means, "Now, can we proceed?" And that, too,
is not a question.
... Are you happy with that?
The Adjudicator has refused refugee status for you.
... Are you happy with that?
You are to be evicted from your accommodation and you
face deportation.
... Are you happy with that?
Now, this paragraph is you, sign here, and here, thank you.
You will hear from me shortly, you need not do anything,
just leave it all to me.
... Are you happy with that?

Geography for beginners

I am from Palestine. I don't want money. I have learned to live without money. Just show me, where can I sleep? Where can I sleep?

I am from the Sudan ...
>*(Read again from after "Palestine" to the end)*

I am from Congo-Kinshasa ...
>*(Repeat the exercise)*

I am from Ethiopia ...
>*(Get the idea?)*

I am from Iraq ...
>*(You can do it on your own now! Take a map of the world, pick a country at war – civil war, or any other war – and you can practise this exercise in the comfort of your own home. If you do need help, just ask anyone in the queue at the Welsh or Scottish or English Refugee Council, or in any number of similar queues all over the world)*

"Incidents of racism are falling"
(*South Wales Evening Post*, 20 January 2005)

Between the old year and the new, in the very first seconds of New Year's Day, the whole family was happy, celebrating with my old father, visiting from Kabylia, my wife and me and our three children, everyone chatting, then there was this horrible noise on the front door. We froze. Again, this horrible noise on the front door. Just moments after midnight. The children screamed, my wife was scared, my father fell silent.

I went to the door, my children behind me, my father behind me. Right in front of me, he was standing there, a drunk youth standing there with a big stone in his hands. Fuck you! he shouted. The others were a few houses further down the road, a gang of youths shouting obscenities. There was something missing in their behaviour. They were pounding the tarmac with big stones. I was baffled. And then I saw that they had slashed the tyres of my car, broken the mirrors, dented the boot, as well as damaging our front door. I was utterly baffled. The police arrived at lunch time ...

Of course, by now it's a new tyre almost daily, and eggs against the window every night ...

"Incidents of racism are falling" 2

Outside CK's supermarket, High Street, February 2005:
Thumped, kicked, floored, knocked out for six – "Black bitch!"

Language problems

We'd just arrived ... December 2004 ... not yet learned more than a word of English ... My wife was seeing the GP with our baby twins, I was in the waiting room with the two girls playing in the children's corner. One of them finds a purse in the toy box and hands it to me. It burns my fingers! I throw it back down and say "Don't!" in Arabic. A woman gets up, walks over and looks in the box. I guess it must be her purse. I reach down, take it and hand it to her. She rips it out of my hands and gives me a dirty look. I empty all the coins from my pocket and mime: "You count your money, this is mine!" She glares. I tell my daughters to come and sit quietly. Our Arabic seems to infuriate the woman. She storms to the receptionist, speaking and gesturing towards me, then she walks out.

Six weeks later, my case worker sends me a "First Warning for Purse Theft." I've been labelled a thief, without even having a hearing.

Thieves face deportation. I am not a thief. I wish someone would chase this up and clear my name ...

Home early from school

Brown girl
God does not love you
That's why he made you brown
You will be sent to hell
So does my teacher say
So does my mother say
So does my father say
Brown girl!

106

Insomnia

unable to switch off
lights on
eyes wide

The father: Till dawn I pace between four walls. I play with my children's keyboard. I try the bed, I try the settee, I try the floor ... but I don't try the door. Outside, Swansea is dangerous ...

The student: I cry, my lips tremble, I walk down the beach. Sure, I fear for my life, so I write, I write, I write ...

The mother: I cannot go to sleep, I must stay awake, I need to protect my children.

British justice

Two years in Swansea waiting for a date for a Home Office interview – a first interview! Two years on NASS handouts with my wife and children, without any news of my claim.

One afternoon, immigration raids a restaurant where friends of mine work. I was there, passing the time. Course, they didn't believe I wasn't working. A week later, they woke us at six in the morning, came with a van to take us all away. Detention, deportation. They handed me a letter from the Home Office. Claim refused! Never had an interview, never had a hearing, claim refused!

Emancipation

Sister to brother:
Here in the UK, you no longer own me! Cook for yourself!

How to dress in the UK

The French enjoy dressing smart and chic. Here, people don't care how they dress. For me, I shall keep dressing the French way – *la vie est un fardeau!* (Life is such a burden!)

Cruelty

This woman rings at two in the morning, says she's heard the men from Leena Homes and Clearsprings talking, and they're coming to deport me: "Run with your children, NOW!"
So, in my pyjamas, I ran with my babies to the nearest friend's house.
It wasn't true, it was a hoax.
Why DO that to me?

Twinning

The meeting of the Pontardawe–Locminé twinning association was just breaking up. A local man standing near to me spoke to somebody else in such rapid Swansea Valley Wenglish that I could only make out this one sentence: "I AGREEE TO A DEGREEE WITH THE BEE-ENN-PEEE ..."

In My Dreams You All Speak Somali

Dahlian Kirby

He was six when they said that he was to go on the aeroplane first. That's what they said. First. We love you, you are our favourite son and you'll travel to Britain in a big aeroplane all by yourself. You mustn't be afraid. Somalia is no place to live, you'll get no education here, my love. We'll see you soon.

He is tall for his age, thin. But he cannot read or write. Nor can he speak. He stands in the corner of the playground by the wall. His lips are tightly closed. His eyes narrow against the wind as he watches the older children kick a football up and down the playground, younger children scattering.

The bell rings, the children head inside. A teacher dashes into the playground, holding her hand out to him. He stares at the place where the game was played, doesn't seem to notice the teacher. "Come on, Ali, play time is over. Come on, you'll catch your death." He allows himself to be led across the playground and into the warmth.

A meeting is held with Social Services. He still isn't talking, not even in his own language. He eats little at home, nothing at school. He doesn't smile. Worse, he doesn't cry. His foster mother, a Somali lady with eleven children, remains unfazed.

"He won't do any work in class, did you know that?"

"The teacher told me."

"Not even art. Not even PE."

"He is waiting for his parents."

"I thought you'd told him that they're not coming. That you're his mother now."

"I did."

Thinner now, he still stands in the same place, apart from the others. He watches the big boys and girls sliding up and down, till the ice is like glass. Children fall, clothes tear, knees bleed. The children shout and laugh. He suppresses a smile.

The bell rings, the children head inside and are ushered into the assembly hall. Some look puzzled: they already had assembly this morning. Older, wiser children know why they are there: they're in for a telling off.

The head teacher paces and mutters, then shouts across the big Victorian hall. How dare they? How dare they! How dare they slide up and down the playground and make a slide? She shouts, she paces. She looks to the other staff for support. They shake their heads in a way they hope will satisfy her.

He gets cramp in his leg. He uncrosses his legs and stands up to bang the numb leg on the floor. Mid-pace the head stops. She stares at him. Slowly all follow her horrified gaze. The tall thin Somali boy in Mrs Price's class keeps banging his foot on the scuffed parquet floor. Several children gasp with shock. The head teacher, almost frothing at the mouth, wades through the grey-uniformed cross-legged children. They part like the Red Sea as she goes. She stops in front of him. He feels her quaking presence and looks up.

"Ali Mahamoud! My office, now!"

He looks at her blankly.

"Miss, he doesn't speak English," says a Pakistani boy.

"I decide who does and doesn't speak English!" she shrieks. "He's been here since September. Of course he speaks English. He certainly understands English. GET OUT, Ali!"

He sees that she is waving her hands, sees everyone else is still sitting, and presumes that she is telling him to sit down. He sits. As his bottom touches the floor, she grabs his arm. She pulls him through the Red Sea of shocked children, up to the front. There is silence. She thinks she might hyperventilate. Her heart is beating fast. Her hands shake. Beside her, Ali

Mahamoud from Class Four looks noble and calm. Someone dares to giggle.

Pulling Ali by the arm, she walks quickly from the hall. Outside her office she lets go of the long thin arm. She rings his foster mother and tells her that he is a bad boy and must go home for the rest of the day.

He stands watching the older children play football. Someone from his class approaches him, holding out an open bag of crisps. He shakes his head. The ball flies through the air and thuds against the wall, bounces off and into a flowerbed. Ali picks it up. "Throw it!" shouts one of the big girls. But he doesn't throw it. He drops it to the ground and he kicks it towards her. She thanks him, turns away, doesn't see the shadow of a smile that plays on his lips for just a moment.

In the corridor, Ali listens to the children in front of him. He understands some of the words. He goes into class and gets his maths work out. He likes maths. It makes sense.

A meeting is held to discuss Ali's progress, or lack of it. His class teacher defends him. Only this week he got changed for PE. She talks about progress in maths. The head teacher mocks her: "He colours in and copies numbers. Wow!"

His foster mother admits he misbehaves at home. "But after all he had been through ..." she adds, feeling disloyal.

"He kicked someone again yesterday," says the head, in a voice that suggests she is shocked, as if no six-year-old boy had ever kicked anyone before.

"I think he's bright," says his special needs teacher, "which makes it worse."

Outside in the sunshine, a football game is going on. Thirty on one side, twenty-three on the other, they call it Christians v Muslims. There are only two actual Christians in the school. What they mean is Welsh v Somalis, Pakistanis, one Turkish boy and two Indian girls, who in fact are Sikhs, but that doesn't seem to matter. Ali moves away from his safe place near the wall, not taking his eyes off the ball for a second.

Inside the head teacher's office, his foster father clears his throat. "So," says Mr Mahamoud slowly, "what are you going to do?"

The head teacher bangs her fist on the table. "Well, Mr. Mahamoud, what are you going to do?"

"Shall I remind you," says Mr. Mahamoud, "of what my son has been through? He is an asylum seeker. He travelled all the way from some village in Somalia on his own. Alone. At six years old. He has seen terrible things. Who knows what he has seen. He cleans his teeth. He prays to God. He dresses himself. Sometimes he eats his dinner. He is changing for PE. He is copying numbers. He is watching TV with our children."

"He has started to call me mother," adds Mrs. Mahamoud.

"My boy is making great progress," says Mr. Mahamoud proudly. He leans back in his chair, crosses one long thin leg over another and smiles at the head teacher.

How she hates him! The same cheekbones. Same African prince pride. The head teacher likes her ethnic minority parents humble and shy. She likes them without a degree.

Playtime is nearly over. How he longs to give that ball a good hard kick, watch as it flies through the air and scores a goal! See the other children scream with surprise. See them leap in the air and shout "Ali! Ali! Ali!" He itches to join in.

Today the sky is blue. The sun is bathing the playground in bright light. It's boys v girls. The girls are bigger, but the boys are more fearless. Ali stands close, never taking his eyes off the ball. His foster sister kicks the ball, then turns to him.

"Come on Ali, join in." She says it in English. He starts to shake his head. But why not? Why shouldn't he?

Every night he lies in bed thinking of his Mum and Dad and brothers and sisters. The ones in Somalia. He thinks they don't need him and don't love him. He used to dream about them. Now he dreams about school and Mrs Price and football, his new Mum and Dad and the new mosque and the chip shop and things he's seen on TV.

A boy in his foster sister's class approaches him.

"Come on Ali! Come and play."

Ali shakes his head.

"Do you understand me?" asks the boy.

Ali shakes his head. He wants to say, "Do you understand me? Does anyone understand who I am?" But he doesn't.

Ali shakes his head and walks away. In his dreams he plays. In his dreams he scores goal after goal. In his dreams they all like him. In his dreams they all understand him. In his dreams they all speak Somali.

The boy is about to turn back to the game. But something about Ali's slight hesitation stops him. He isn't Ali, but he feels that he used to be. He came from Afghanistan when he was about Ali's age. He couldn't speak English either. He'd felt angry because they all spoke a language that wasn't his. The ball is kicked his way. The boy from Afghanistan controls the ball and kicks it towards Ali. It hits Ali on the back of the leg. Ali turns, ready to hit who ever has done this to him. The boy from Afghanistan, who isn't Ali but used to be, smiles and indicates that Ali should kick the ball.

He kicks the ball. Ali kicks the ball with a kick that is strong and firm and powerful. The ball sails through the air at half speed and is kicked again and then again. The ball is back in the game and now Ali is there too, running, kicking, struggling to breathe and keep pace with the bigger children. Up and down the school yard they all run. Little ones scatter. The bell rings, the running stops. His heart banging against his ribs, Ali walks towards the school door. The footballers are talking about the game. Ali is nodding and saying "yeah, yeah" with all the others.

As he walks down the corridor, the head teacher's office door opens. Out come his teacher and his parents, who have been called to the school for the second time in a week. His mother hugs him. He doesn't push her away. His foster sister says, "Ali joined in the football." Ali's father smiles. His teacher smiles. A boy whose name Ali doesn't know says: "Want to play at dinner time, Ali?" Ali says: "Yeah." Ali's father shakes his teacher's hand. Ali feels something incredible is happening.

Ali plays football every break time and every lunchtime, on his way home from school, and at weekends. He sometimes plays after mosque, if his Mum says he can. He wants to tell the whole world how wonderful football is. He wants to tell the children. He wants to tell them his dreams, the ones he has when he's safe asleep in bed, and the ones he thinks as he walks to school or gazes out of the classroom window. He will talk to his friends about football and PE and school dinners. But he will never ever tell them the most wonderful thing about his dreams, the dreams where he plays football for Cardiff City and scores goal after goal, and they all shout his name: in his dreams, you all speak Somali.

Less Than Dust

Martin J. White

Blindly a breeze winds
off water over land
cleaves to contours
and ruffles a far forest
or meeting fences
flows through man-made mesh
dust going with it
fry too fine
to gather in a net

A newspaper catches
folds then wraps
cruel razored strands
with witnessed wounds of war
fact of famine
what makes refuge imperative
but news has gone global
a gust gets it through

A bird finds no barrier
watchful wire-walker
he chooses where to rest
only people poor are held
not to have a freedom
natural to birds
to breezes
our needs become old news
and what are we
to those who rule us?

Peace / Praise / Winter

Alhaji Sheku Kamara = ASK

Peace

Since I was a small boy I've been searching for peace, I've seen a lot of bloodshed and killing and I survived a bloody war, yet still peace is nowhere to be found. I wonder why.

Yesterday has gone, tomorrow is unknown, but today is here, the sun is dying and the place is getting dark and my search is getting more difficult as I don't know where to find Mr Hawk, the warlord of the world.

The cock has crowed "Ko-koriyoko!" – a new day is born. I think of Mr Dove, the peaceful man. I went to see him to see if he can bring peace into the world. I rely on him because he is a world superpower, but he let me down because he was crying over not succeeding in giving the world peace.

I was about to give up but Mr Parrot met us and gave Mr Dove some advice which gave me courage. He said to him: You can't extinguish a fire with fire and you can't achieve peace without giving me and the people of the world what we want. We don't want violence for the sake of peace, all we want is love, equal rights, justice and unconditional inter-racial brotherly and sisterly love. That's what we call peace.

Praise

To all who are helping refugees and asylum seekers in the UK

Praise be to the most high almighty God the greatest, and special thanks to all those who are helping the poor and needy in different ways – Big Up! Yeah! – I was dumped in the bin like rubbish that's not supposed to be in a house, but thanks be to the rubbish collector who took me out and gave me soap and clean water to wash myself – because he knew very well that I am a human being like him, not what the ones who dumped me think I am.

I am prevented from finding food to feed myself, so I will starve, but thanks be to the people who provide me with food, and praise be to the master of creation, God, who gave them the strength and courage to help me.

Stress was trying to take my life away but thanks be to the good people who helped me through. Please keep up the good work. I know you will not stop even if they set a roadblock, because they can't keep a good man nor a good woman down.

Winter

The sun is shining and the weather is nice, nice and warm. Women in their fancy clothes looking very attractive and men in their designer gear enjoying the weather.

But soon, soon the wind, the wind will start to undress the trees and leave them naked. Everybody will become a bluffer with their hands in their pockets. Slim people will become fat, and fat people extra fat as thick jumpers and coats build up their bodies, as if they were going to the gym. Some people imitate goalkeepers and boxers by putting on big gloves.

Everybody will become a singer, singing the single of the season:

It's very cold today
It's freezing inni'?
Yeah I'm freezing
It might be snow tomorrow.
This is winter, we should expect that.

117

Pain in the Neck

Anahita Alikhani

Trouble and trouble makers in the UK

"Trouble" is a small word with just two syllables, but a large meaning. Like the rain in the UK, it never stops. Anything can be trouble – something natural, something strange, something complex, something simple.

But "trouble makers" is two words, with just one meaning: asylum seekers. They travel across the whole world to come to the UK and cause all the trouble in this country. They are like the Huns or Vandals of history who destroyed everything and left nothing behind. Asylum seekers are like locusts: they chew everything – even British people's nerves.

Who likes trouble? Nobody.

Most of the time, the UK is damp, dark, cloudy and rainy. According to the newspapers, since the time when asylum seekers started to come to the UK, even the sky feels pity for the British people, and so the sky weeps every day.

What happened to the British colonies? Asylum seekers took them from the UK, then they started coming over here.

The price of petrol is going up again next week – but if we kicked out all the Middle Eastern asylum seekers and sent them back to their countries to produce oil, we could give them just a little money, instead of paying lots of money to British workers, and then the price of petrol would stay low.

But the asylum seekers want to be here, alive and vertical, rather than be there, dead and horizontal.

British citizens pay more than 25% tax on their earnings – that's because asylum seekers have furnished houses. Homelessness is an increasing problem here – that's because asylum seekers have taken all the houses.

When you can't get a seat on the train – when the bus is late – when the roads are jammed with traffic – when somebody doesn't get elected to parliament – when somebody does get elected to parliament – when somebody gets drunk and falls over in the street – when you wake up in the morning with a hangover – when your football team loses – when you buy a new pair of shoes and they pinch – who is to blame for all these things?!

ASYLUM SEEKERS!!

Interview with a foreigner

To find a job in the UK is even harder than getting status as a refugee. A job interview is even tougher than a Home Office interview. In the Home Office, as long as you didn't make up your case, it is not too difficult to answer all the questions. In a job interview, the questions are bizarre and you don't know how you're supposed to answer them.

The main points in a job interview will be: what do you wear, what do you look like, which part of the world do you come from, what is your religion, etcetera. The right answers depend on the person asking the questions. They always smile, trying to show that they are nice people; they try to fool you with their attitude, and with me they always succeed. The smiles mean: you're never going to get this job. If they seem happy, it's a very very bad sign.

This is an imaginary job interview – slightly exaggerated but based on experience.

I put my bottom on the chair and try hard to concentrate, remembering my friend's advice: Don't show how clever you are! Answer their questions with questions! Let them think you are stupid! Take a moment after the question before replying! Don't give a straight answer!

First they show their sympathy:

– Do you need anything? Tea, coffee?

– No, thank you.

Then the four of them start taking turns to ask questions:

– Could you tell us about yourself?

– Actually everything is on the CV.

– We didn't see anything about your father and mother. Can you tell us about your ancestry?

– Sorry, I didn't know I'd be expected to introduce you to my ancestors.

– What are your ambitions?

(They always ask this and I don't know what to answer. If I say I have great ambitions, they'll think I am a trouble-maker. If I tell them about small ambitions, they'll say: Sorry, our firm is a very big firm and we need a person with great ambitions. I stutter, playing for time.)

– Actually, at the moment my great ambition is to find a job.

– Why have you chosen to apply here?

– Same reason as you did.

– What do you have to offer our company?

– What do you want? You have the right to choose. You tell me what I should do for you.

– How long have you been here?

– Three years.

– Excellent. You have excellent English. Were you able to talk English before you came here?

(God I hate this. This is a very bad sign. They are starting to play with me.)

– No. I learned here.

– Oh, then you have time to practise your English.

– Thank you very much.

– Do you like it here? What about the people?

– Of course, I love being here. The people are very nice and friendly.

(Except for the job interviewers, I think to myself.)

– Do you know anything about the history of Wales?

– Yes. A bit. I can't say I'm an expert but I know something.

– Do you know anything about mine problems?

– Sorry, I don't know anything about your problems.

– No, not my problems, I mean mine problems.

– Ah, yes, mines, they explode if you put your foot on them.

– No, no, mines, coalmines.

– Oh, I'm sorry, I couldn't understand your Welsh accent. You mean in the 60s, the mine problems?

– Yes.

– I watched a documentary about that once, that's all I know.

– Do you know how many schools there are in Wales?

– Oh god, no, I don't.

– OK, how many universities?

– Five or four I think, I'm not sure.

– What are you doing at the moment?

– A job interview.

– No, I mean in your spare time.

– Studying English, writing, painting ...

– Why have you chosen this job? You know you have a very strong accent.

– You too!

(He smiles very nicely. I think, oh god, another disaster, I'm not going to get this job. He looks at me very kindly, and asks:)

– Do you really want this job?

– I really love this job. This is my dream.

– Do you want this job? Then answer this question, and I'll give you the job.

– What's the question?

– What was the name of my father's dog?

From Nothing to Something

Michael Mokako

Here I am thinking about how I will achieve my dreams
Struggling day to day trying to arrange a good future
I know a day will come when things will go my way
I can just feel the shine, soon it's going to be my time

I can feel myself travelling from nothing to something
Sometimes people try to bring me down but I ain't scared
Because nobody is stopping me following my dreams
Even if they say I'll never make it, whatever they say

Isn't going to put me down, I know one day I'll make it
Not today, not tomorrow, but one day, I'll win all the respect
That has been taken and I'll become somebody

No matter what it's going to take
No matter what people are saying, I'll make it
Then I'll move from nothing to something

PATCHWORK PROJECT

If you're a postgraduate Scientist, Health Worker or Engineer, and you're having difficulty finding the right job, then this could be the project for you!

The project is aimed at postgraduate Scientists, Health Workers and Engineers, who have been out of the workplace due to relocation (refugees) or domestic responsibilities (women and men returnees).

You may have a need to prove qualification equivalence, or have a lack of knowledge of recent and emerging technologies. Relatively well-qualified women and men can find it difficult to return to work after a period of domestic responsibilities, because the workplace has changed.

The idea of the project is to 'patch' these skills and up-date needs to enable a successful return to work.

The courses will be available for two days a week, but support will be available every week day.

PLACES ARE LIMITED

For further information, please contact **Shahid Altaf** or **Judith James**:
Tel: 01792 295382 / 295795   /   *Fax*: 01792 295751
Email: s.altaf@swansea.ac.uk / j.james@swansea.ac.uk
Department of Adult Continuing Education,
University of Wales Swansea, SA2 8PP

www.swan.ac.uk/dace/newdace/tv/patchworks.asp

EUROPEAN COMMUNITY
European Social Fund
Y GYMUNED EWROPEAIDD
Cronfa Gymdeithasol Ewrop

WELSH LOCAL AUTHORITIES CONSORTIUM FOR REFUGEES AND ASYLUM SEEKERS

The Welsh Local Authorities Consortium (WLACRAS) includes amongst its members local authorities in the four dispersal areas of Wales (Cardiff, Newport, Swansea and Wrexham), the Welsh Assembly Government, the British Red Cross, the Welsh Refugee Council and other statutory and voluntary agencies across Wales.

The Consortium works together to develop a multi-agency approach to meeting the diverse housing, health, educational, social, cultural, linguistic and religious needs of asylum seekers, as well as to enable longer-term settlement for those granted leave to remain, humanitarian protection or refugee status.

In carrying out this work the Consortium recognises the challenges which we face together within a complex and fast-changing legislative and political framework.

The Consortium and its member agencies continually strive to work closely with refugees and asylum seekers to offer the welcome and support that they need.

We also recognise the unique qualities, experience and resilience of asylum seekers and refugees and the extent to which they enrich our Welsh culture and society.

Contacts

Manager: Anne Hubbard
Project Funding Officer: Aled Singleton

WLACRAS
Brynglas Bungalow
Brynglas Road
Newport
NP20 5QU

Tel: 01633 855095

AWEMA

MAINSTREAMING FROM THE MARGINS

The All Wales Ethnic Minority Association (AWEMA) congratulates SBASSG, Hafan Books and Refugee Week Wales on this publication. *AWEMA works to develop the capacity of community groups in a range of areas:*

- *Engaging hard-to-reach individuals, households, communities*
- *Raising awareness of the Welsh Assembly Government's policy and strategy, as it affects our communities*
- *Engaging Welsh BME civil society with UK-wide civil society*
- *Developing the capacity of community groups and organisations on issues of international development*

Suite 1.2, 1St Floor
St David's House
Wood Street
Cardiff
CF10 1ES

Tel.: 029 2066 4213
Fax: 029 2023 6071
admin@awema.freeserve.co.uk
Registered Company Number 4114532
Registered Charity Number 1108479

Some Other Local Charities

Displaced People in Action (Cardiff)	Tel. 029 2041 5706
British Red Cross (Swansea)	Tel. 01792 772146
SOVA ('Plethu' volunteer mentors project)	Tel. 029 2049 5281
Minority Ethnic Women's Network (Swansea)	Tel. 01792 467722
Swansea Bay Race Equality Council	Tel. 01792 457035
Amnesty International (Swansea)	Tel. 07967509590
Medical Foundation (South West Wales Supporters Group)	
	Tel. 01792 232224
Asylum Justice / Croeso	Tel. 07968177564

 **refugee** week
wales

Refugee Week is a unique opportunity to celebrate the enormous contributions that refugees and asylum seekers make to the UK, and to try and promote understanding about why people become refugees.

Refugee Week was developed in response to the increasingly negative perceptions and misunderstanding of refugees and asylum seekers held by the general public. This is despite the fact that Refugee communities have made enormous social, economic and cultural contributions to Wales and the UK. Fish and chips, the Mini and Marks and Spencer are all British institutions - created or invented by refugees who came to the UK.

During Refugee Week, lots of events take place across Wales, organised by charities, local government, refugee community organisations, faith based organisations, schools and arts organisations. These events can be large or small, and include arts events such as concerts, exhibitions and festivals; sporting activities; events in schools; local community events and seminars and discussions around key issues.

You can show your support for Refugee Week 2006 by organising an event in your local area, or getting involved with existing activities.

If you're new to Refugee Week and want to find out more, for ideas about events, or to find out what is happening around Wales, contact the Refugee Week Team at the Welsh Refugee Council on:

Tel: 029 2043 2990 Email info@refugeeweekwales.org
Web:www.refugeeweekwales.org
and www.refugeeweek.org.uk

Refugee Week 2006 will take place from 19th to 26th June